Human-Driven Experience

Human-Driven Experience

The Battle for Trust in the Digital Age

Robert Harles

WILEY

This edition first published 2023

Copyright © 2023 by Robert Harles

Registered office

John Wiley & Sons Ltd, The Atrium, Southern Gate, Chichester, West Sussex, PO19 8SQ, United Kingdom

For details of our global editorial offices, for customer services and for information about how to apply for permission to reuse the copyright material in this book please see our website at www.wiley.com.

Wiley publishes in a variety of print and electronic formats and by print-on-demand. Some material included with standard print versions of this book may not be included in e-books or in print-on-demand. If this book refers to media such as a CD or DVD that is not included in the version you purchased, you may download this material at http://booksupport.wiley.com. For more information about Wiley products, visit www.wiley.com.

Designations used by companies to distinguish their products are often claimed as trademarks. All brand names and product names used in this book are trade names, service marks, trademarks or registered trademarks of their respective owners. The publisher is not associated with any product or vendor mentioned in this book.

Limit of Liability/Disclaimer of Warranty: While the publisher and author have used their best efforts in preparing this book, they make no representations or warranties with respect to the accuracy or completeness of the contents of this book and specifically disclaim any implied warranties of merchantability or fitness for a particular purpose. It is sold on the understanding that the publisher is not engaged in rendering professional services and neither the publisher nor the author shall be liable for damages arising herefrom. If professional advice or other expert assistance is required, the services of a competent professional should be sought.

Library of Congress Cataloging-in-Publication Data

Names: Harles, Robert, author.
Title: Human-driven experience : the battle for trust in the digital age / by Robert Harles.
Description: [Hoboken, New Jersey] : Wiley, 2023. | Includes index.
Identifiers: LCCN 2022029459 (print) | LCCN 2022029460 (ebook) | ISBN 9781119812982 (hardback) | ISBN 9781119813002 (adobe pdf) | ISBN 9781119812999 (epub)
Subjects: LCSH: Consumer behavior. | Consumption (Economics) | Branding (Marketing)
Classification: LCC HF5415.32 .H375 2022 (print) | LCC HF5415.32 (ebook) | DDC 658.8/342—dc23/eng/20220707
LC record available at https://lccn.loc.gov/2022029459
LC ebook record available at https://lccn.loc.gov/2022029460

Cover Design: Wiley
Cover Image: © pialhovik/Getty Images
Printed and bound by CPI Group (UK) Ltd, Croydon, CR0 4YY

C9781119812982_150922

To my wife, Becky, whose kindness, thoughtfulness, and desire to serve others reminds me every day what it means to be truly human. To my daughters, Violette and Collette, who motivate me to do more to make the world just a little bit better. To my parents, Walter and Jeanette, whose love, support, and patience know no bounds.

Contents

Introduction: Power to the People

Nothing eases suffering like the human touch.

—Bobby Fischer

As a society, we are at a momentous crossroads. The past 30 years have seen tremendous growth in the areas of technology, data, and capital, although this growth hasn't always been smooth. It's the fundamental struggle for economic growth and social stability.

This same struggle has played out throughout history, but what is different about today is that our old controls, structures, processes, and understanding are failing us in the face of unprecedented change. Before, change happened slowly over time, giving people and businesses a chance to change and adapt to what was coming. Now, we face rapid-fire changes in technology, societal norms, and government policies, and we must adapt to the changing environments in the blink of an eye. There is nowhere to hide. Technology, data, and forces beyond our control have conspired to challenge us professionally, politically, socially, and emotionally.

I have arrived at a point in my career at which I believe I have a pretty good idea of where data, technology, and next-generation _____ (fill in the blank) are going, at least superficially. But I also realize that this is not the whole picture; there is something more beneath the surface that is absolutely critical to understand if we are to survive, adapt, and thrive in this new world. Exactly how I got to this realization is an interesting question, because the path I took in my own career was a counterintuitive one.

When I finished college 25 years ago with a master's degree in history, I hadn't a clue what I would do with it. If I look back to the way the world was then versus the way it is today, it is virtually unrecognizable—particularly from a technology perspective. The iPhone was still a decade away from being introduced, Google didn't yet exist, and General Motors was about to pull the plug on its pioneering EV1 electric car. The dot-com bubble was quickly inflating, and investors were bullish on most any company that had a presence on the web— whether or not it could actually turn a profit. Remember Webvan and Pets.com?

When I was in high school, I dabbled with computers and did a little programming—nothing out of the ordinary. My original plan was to major in architectural history in college, but I eventually settled on modern European history, which covers the period starting in the late seventh century and runs up to the coming of war in the early 1930s.

Perfect choice for someone who is now responsible for helping develop Accenture's digital offerings in social media and emerging channels, right?

Okay—please bear with me for a moment.

Despite my choice of a major, my college experience shaped my thoughts about technology and business for the rest of my life. I was offered the chance to run the business club at Oxford, which was called the Industrial Society. Fearing unemployment, it was a chance I gratefully jumped at. That's where I was first introduced to business and to companies—everything from consulting to engineering to consumer goods.

The *raison d'être* of the Industrial Society was to help students make connections with potential employers. And since there were no business-related degree programs at Oxford at the time—as you might imagine, the school was heavy on English literature, languages, classics, politics, philosophy, economics, and the like. The Industrial Society was popular with students who were thinking of starting a career in business after graduation.

I believe we were one of the first student clubs at Oxford University that had a web page, and chances are, we were probably one of the first student organizations *anywhere* that had its own web page. Still, I am not sure that the importance of that moment really dawned on me at the time. I had no idea how quickly events would over overtake the world and how in only a few short years a web page might spawn a whole new economy.

As I wrapped up my degree in modern European history, the topic of what I should do with the rest of my life was starting to gain some urgency. My parents were especially concerned, particularly when I said I was giving serious consideration to a career as an academic in architectural history.

At the same time, I was organizing yet another recruiting event at Oxford for a consultancy, this time on behalf of McKinsey. I was always organizing these kinds of events, but for some reason I never went to them as a guest. This time, however, the McKinsey recruiter asked me, "You've been organizing all these recruiting events—why don't you come and I will introduce you to a few folks?"

Why *didn't* I go? Good question.

So, I decided to go to the McKinsey event I had organized, and I ended up applying for a job with the firm. I didn't know anything about management consulting, and I really didn't think my application was going to go anywhere given my complete and utter lack of business, economic, or technology credentials.

One thing led to another, however, and I was scheduled for a round of interviews where seemingly every question was a case study about how many pennies there are in the United States or how to boost the circulation of newspapers in Norway. There was only one opening in my cohort, and I was up against a high number of very qualified candidates—some already working as analysts, plus a smattering of Rhodes and Fulbright Scholars. I didn't think I had a snowball's chance.

The day of the final interview, I stood up, thanked the interviewer, and said my goodbyes to the recruiter, confident that I would not receive an offer. I remember being subdued when my parents asked me how it went. We were about to go out to dinner to commiserate when the phone rang. The recruiter on the other end said nothing about how I did in the interviews but asked me if I would be attending the "offer dinner" in London. I asked what dinner she was referring to, to which she replied, "Oh my goodness, let me have someone call you right back!" She then hung up.

Two minutes later (which seemed an eternity), another recruiter called and let me know they were making me an offer. My head was buzzing, so I missed everything else she said after that. I just remember saying yes.

Later, when I attended the offer dinner, I met up with one of my interviewers. I asked why they had made me an offer (still sounding a bit incredulous in my mind—clearly, they must have made a mistake?). Luckily, the question seemed to come off as simply inquisitive. He told me that everyone liked how my mind worked, that having a historian's perspective would be an advantage when working with clients that often had to deal with short-term issues but sometimes wanted a perspective on the long game.

I really enjoyed working at McKinsey, but in 1998—after just a few years there—some of my friends and I decided to start up our own company. Our vision was to develop web-based financial planning applications for retail financial services institutions, but our unique twist was to make these tools much more accessible to the end user—ordinary customers.

We were on to something. A number of our clients were trying to reach burgeoning investors and bank customers who didn't know nor care what a Monte Carlo simulation was but did want to know if they should buy life insurance or an annuity. After some fraught sales cycles, we started to sign up fee-paying clients—retail banks and credit unions. All signals indicated that we were on the right path (making financial services accessible and more self-serve for consumers). The financial model made sense: licensing plus lead generation to major financial instructions. What could go wrong?

Then the dot-com bubble burst and funding dried up. That could have been the end but it turned out to be a transformational experience nonetheless. I could have gone back to school for a business degree, but the years I spent building a start-up were invaluable. I took a significantly deeper dive into technology, I learned how to put a business plan together, how to make pitches to angel investors and venture capital and private equity firms, and I figured out how to secure partnerships with major companies and content providers. Above all, the experience let me put into practice and validate lessons learned about the importance of treating employees, vendors, clients, and customers as "people." Little did I know how important that lesson would become.

It was at that point that I got the technology and innovation bug—*bad*.

We sold the company in 2001, and I went back to consulting at another firm where my job was to apply some of the lessons I learned and drive profitable growth strategies for Fortune 500 clients. This is also where I got an appreciation for understanding the nature of demand. After a few years, I accepted an offer to become a senior vice president at an online data company, where I led the firm's retail, technology, and travel digital analytics business. By this time, I had developed a very technical bent. It had quickly become a 24/7 kind of thing for me.

A few years into my tenure, I was working on a client project focused on building a new loyalty program, when one day the lead client asked me, "Since you architected this community program for us, how would you like to come on board full time and run it?" The company was Sears, and at the time it was still in the midst of a hoped-for turnaround. It was also still a really big deal—one of the largest retailers on the planet. I wasn't sure what it was I would be doing, but it seemed like I could build something from scratch and was at the intersection of my two passions: technology and people. I jumped at the offer.

I became a vice president within their digital group and head of Social Media and Community. Working directly with customers and hearing their stories first hand was eye opening and was the first time I really started thinking about the importance of some basic self-evident truths, such as, if you want to build loyalty and long-lasting relationships, you need to build trust. And no matter what channel or technology your customers use, trust is predicated on a fundamental principle: all customers are people who want to feel they matter. This one idea has colored the rest of my career.

When, a few years later, I built the social media program at Bloomberg, I tried to apply the same vision. Instead of using new technologies and channels to broadcast and talk to customers, we used them to understand their needs, interests, and concerns in real time. One of the things that attracted me to Bloomberg was its culture, particularly the seeming flatness of organization. Since there were no structural barriers or walls in any of the offices, there was no real obstacle to meeting, talking, sharing ideas with people—from analysts, to the talent, to the CEO and chairman.

I remember one of the best pieces of advice I ever received, which made me think about the importance of focusing on people first. My first week at Bloomberg, I felt a bit lost. I had passion for the job before me, I had plan, and I had support, but I was struggling with where to begin. Should I jump in and just start organizing meetings with all the senior execs to extoll the virtues of social media—explaining how it could transform their business—or should I pick off a few small projects and demonstrate the power of modern channels out of the gate? I wanted to move fast and demonstrate value.

Luckily, I "bumped" into Bloomberg chairman Peter Grauer as I walked past his desk one day. He immediately said a hello and asked me how I was settling in. I told him about my plan and how quickly I wanted to move. Peter struck me as very old school, partly because his career forced him to build deep relationships, but mostly because I think he is a people person—kind and caring. He listened impassively, and when I was done explaining how I planned to conquer the world, he said, "Before you do all that, just take whatever time you need to sit down with people and really get to know them, understand what motivates them. Don't even talk about what *you* want to do, ask questions and find out what *they* are looking to do."

So simple, but often something we all have trouble doing whether talking with friends, colleagues, customers, or clients. I was told when I first started as a consultant that I needed to speak up more, that clients paid us for our thoughts and counsel. In fact, to hammer home the point, one partner said, "If a consultant is quiet, it's not because they are listening, they are just reloading." But Peter's advice stuck with me, and it must have worked. About two years into my tenure at Bloomberg, while Peter was speaking with the head of sales about the impact of social media on the business, the head of sales paused and told the room that all his salespeople were now using social to connect, interact with, and generate leads from their customers. The listening paid off.

In 2014, my wife and were expecting our second child, and a condition of moving to New York was that we would eventually move back to Chicago to be closer to our families. At about that time, a former colleague approached me and asked if I might come back to consulting and doing for other clients what I was doing for Bloomberg. After some fraught soul searching, I accepted and took a role with Accenture Song. This is where I finally got a chance to push the envelope in terms of using technology, data, and some of the softer people skills to build better and more human and purpose-driven experiences. I also got to use my bent for history more than ever.

With each new job, I got deeper into tech and digital, but always with an eye to understanding how to apply those innovations to understanding people better. Looking back, I can see how my original college interest in history served me well throughout my career. It gave me a sense of how to be inquisitive and push on things. Above all, history's focus on people—their stories, motivations, biases, fears, aspirations, and journeys—stood me in good stead as I navigated the world of business.

And in my case, it's looking at the story arc of *technology* over the past couple of hundred years, looking through a historian's lens on digital. Each of the major technology revolutions we humans have sparked has been a major inflection point in our history—moving us ever forward to places we never imagined possible.

The Agricultural Revolution turned us from hunters and gatherers into builders of cities and complex societies. The Industrial Revolution drew people from farms to factories as new technologies such as steam engines, the telegraph, the Bessemer steelmaking process, and more changed the world forever. The Medical Revolution extended the expected lifetime of humans—in the United States from an average of about 47 years for those born in 1900 to an average of about 77 years for those born in 2000.[1]

The Electronic Revolution led to ever more capable—yet smaller and less expensive—electronic devices based on transistors, which replaced bulky and fragile glass vacuum tubes, and other innovations. The Digital Revolution has brought us to where we are today—holding in our hand compact digital devices that are faster and far more capable than the old IBM mainframes from decades ago that filled a room. And the AI Revolution, where digital devices are able to think like humans, is taking us to where we'll go tomorrow.

The common thread through all these revolutions has been the initial struggles and ultimate triumph of human factor, but each has taken less time than its predecessor. The most recent one—the AI Revolution, which is still emerging—similarly promises to make our lives better while it threatens to de-humanize society. It will either turn out to be a triumphant celebration of humanity's ingenuity and creativity, or an indictment of our collective hubris and folly. Only time will tell.

As a historian, you learn to be critical and not necessarily accept at face value what people tell you. You always have to understand where they're coming from. That empathy piece is critically important—both when I was studying history in school, and when I map out Accenture's digital offerings today. Ultimately, everything we do is meant to make people feel good—to feel confident, satisfied, and even happy to interact with the digital programs we design for our clients across every industry, B2C and B2B. It's as much about understanding human nature as it is about understanding what the needs and desires of customers are.

Since time immemorial, marketers have wrestled with the fact that as they try to figure out where the road is going to take them—where the market is going, where customers are going—they've had to look through the rearview mirror and can only see where they've already been with any degree of accuracy. The correct answer can only be found at the intersection of a lot of different pieces, and ultimately, that's why I wrote this book.

I think a lot of people want to have tactical answers to immediate problems. That's not really what this book is about. I wrote this book with the hope that it will get you to reconsider your perspectives when it comes to digital, invigorate what you do day to day, and maybe pull you out of the status quo that you've been comfortable in for so long. I also provide you with the tools you need to break through the walls that we've put up—sometimes internal, sometimes external—between us and our customers. And if you do that, you will open up an entirely new range of opportunities and possibilities.

Finally, I'm hoping that this book will influence how most effectively to use this thing we call *digital*—the technologies we have already created, as well as the ones we have yet to create—and use them in the aid of humanity. Lofty goals, I know, but it's time for us to stop looking at the rearview mirror to chart our course forward, and to start looking through our windshield instead.

I keep an eye on start-ups as much as I do the companies I work with. I think one of the greatest things about start-ups is that necessity is truly the mother of invention. If you don't have tons of resources to pay for the marketing data and analysis you need, you have to create them the best you can. And that forces you to think about what you can do—how you can push the envelope with what you have.

A few start-ups I've been watching—and personally using—include Decorist, Havenly, and Modsy. They are relatively small start-ups that ask the question: How can we take the whole process of home interior design and make it more egalitarian and use technology and digital to build a collaborative relationship with customers? In other words, how can we humanize an experience that is very much an online one and make customers *love* it?

With these services, you don't pay thousands of dollars for one-to-one interior design service, as you would if you hired your own architect or dedicated designer. Instead, for a relatively small sum of money (a multiroom package currently runs into a few hundred dollars), you can get almost unlimited design advice. They are betting that you're going to like their design recommendations so much that you will buy furniture and other items from their site, and they take their margin off those purchases.

Working with these start-ups is typically a simple step-by-step process that mirrors the kind of human interactions you would have with a real-life architect or designer. First, you can take photos of the room you want to redecorate and then you upload the photos to their design site. They then take your photos, virtually clear out the clutter, and create a to-scale 3D rendering of the room.

The next step is to fill out a style quiz that tells these services more about you—the kinds of questions an architect or designer would ask you in real life. Things such as your budget, your style preferences (for example, modern versus rustic), how open you are to new ideas, and so on. They take the results of this mini-psychographic Q and A and use them as the basis of the personalized design ideas they create just for you.

The final step begins when these design services create an interactive, 3D rendering of your room, with lots of design packages and options for you to consider. The designs are yours to keep, whether or not you purchase any of the furniture or décor items you're offered.

While much of these experiences are digital, there *is* a human element involved—regardless of what package you buy, you are assigned an "expert" designer. This mash-up definitely works, combining the best of digital and human with great results. They also get to really know a customer on a deeper level because the customer feels comfortable sharing their real interests, preferences, and vision. They also share contextual information that exists nowhere else: their living space, their cherished possessions, their true motivations, things typically locked way in designers' and architects' heads when the project is done.

Of course, not every online platform based on digital leaves customers feeling so happy and satisfied. In fact, many end up frustrating customers—leaving them angry instead of happy, an outcome every company wants to avoid. The good news is that business leaders can do something about this.

At Accenture, we talk about the difference between customer experience (CX—optimizing customer touchpoints around products and services) and the business of experience (BX—solving for human needs around a purpose). Our research shows that, on average, BX leaders outperform CX-oriented companies in year-on-year profitability growth by 6.5x over one year, 6.4x over three years, 6.4x over five years, and 6.3x over seven years.[2] Long story short, linking customers to purpose makes a tremendous impact on the bottom line.

Marketers must think beyond simply getting somebody to buy something to also getting them to come back, while thinking about the issues along the line that need to be overcome to engineer the experience from an empathetic standpoint. Not losing the sale because they haven't thought about the things that get in the way of someone saying *yes*. Companies that do this well will use technology smartly to humanize their storyline end to end. They're the companies that are going to win.

This book is all about using technology in smart ways to create empathetic and human digital experiences. In Chapter 1, I tell the story of my childhood customer experience at Marshall Fields, the legendary Chicago department store where I first learned about the importance of the human touch in retail experiences.

In Chapter 2, I consider why we should bother to humanize digital, where digital gets it right, and where digital gets it wrong. I do a deep dive into what makes humans human, and why people want their digital buying experiences to mirror their in-person buying experiences.

In Chapter 3, I propose the idea of creating a new role for CEOs in organizations: the *chief community officer*. This person has remit over the entire organization—to be able to say, "Stop!" whenever customers are suffering because of a company's products or services, or the way they are being delivered doesn't meet the brand's promise. This, I believe, is the starting point for changing the way all the different operational organizational elements work—sales, marketing, and so on.

In Chapter 4, I explain why really focusing on trust above all is the key to the next wave of growth. We'll examine the original digital vision and how it diverged from its intent—undermining trust—the threat to our markets and capitalism itself, and the digital law of diminishing returns.

In Chapter 5, I explain that many of the answers to our questions can be found in our past. What obstacles have impeded our ability to build human empathy into digital systems? How should we frame the problem and solution? What are customers and citizens looking for and what are their concerns? In this chapter, I address these questions and more.

In Chapter 6, I introduce the six pillars of purpose-driven experience. How you get your purpose into an organization and how you get people to align with it is critically important for it to become something that's real—more than just heartwarming words and photos splashed across your website. And this takes an effort that is both bottom-up and top-down. The six pillars provide a framework for accomplishing this effort.

In Chapter 7, I offer a practical guide for readers to humanize digital in their organizations. This guide includes integrating the human dimension into the entire path (e.g., sales reps, distributors, channel partners, etc.); structuring the enterprise for digital trust; ensuring security, compliance, and governance; protecting your brand reputation; managing communications and PR, and much more.

In Chapter 8, I show how to fully realize the vision for digital trust. I consider what we need to put in place and what we need our leaders to do; building a digital trust environment with our people, skills, and resources; taking an organizational design and governance approach; adopting a reputational model that builds greater transparency; and getting everyone on the same page.

In Chapter 9, I provide you with a proven, six-part framework for implementing trust-based empathetic design in your organization—gaining the benefits and reaping the rewards. You can't execute if you don't have a roadmap for where you should take your team and your organization, and in this chapter, I provide you with one that you can quickly put to good use.

In Chapter 10, the last chapter of this book, I leave you with a final call to arms for humanizing our businesses. I show you where the money is, why this will drive operational efficiencies and growth, the value that can be derived, and why the C-suite needs to take this topic seriously and promote top-down change.

We need better understand how building humanity into our digital experiences is critical to meet the needs of our customers, employees, and citizens who are increasingly concerned about the motivations of institutions that embrace technology. This will in turn foster better communication, improve marketing, collaboration, and innovation, buttress democracy, and generate profitable growth. In this book, we address all these challenges—and opportunities—and much more.

Now, let's get started.

Human-Driven Experience

1

What Have Brands Lost Over the Past 30 Years? Recognize, Remember, Recommend, Relevance

No one will protect what they don't care about, and no one will care about what they have never experienced.

—David Attenborough

When I was a kid—and in the context of space and time, it wasn't all that long ago—department stores were a really big deal. And the most notable one in Chicago, where I grew up, was Marshall Field and Company, more commonly known as Marshall Field's. The business was founded in the 1850s, and its flagship store on the corner of State and Washington Streets burned to the ground in the Great Chicago Fire of 1871. The owners rebuilt the store, it burned again in 1877, and the owners again rebuilt—triggering years of growth and profits as the company eventually broke out of its Chicago roots and expanded across the country through numerous acquisitions.

Marshall Field's was always a magical place for a little kid like me because, in the 1970s, the downtown Chicago store's toy department spanned an entire floor. Like every other kid anywhere in the area, I loved to go there. My dad was known by the salespeople in the department because he regularly brought me there to check out the latest offerings (and being an avid model railway enthusiast, he also regularly bought items for himself). As soon as the manager of the department manager spotted my dad, he would make the effort to connect. "Hey Walt," he would say to my dad, "it's good to see you. How have you been? How's the family? You know, something just came in and I haven't even put it out on the floor yet. Your kid's going to love it—I'll go get it."

That was such a uniquely human thing. A salesperson who took the time to get to know us—not just as customers, but as living human beings—and then reach out to us by offering products that he knew we'd be interested in buying. And it seemed like a magical place because you had the feeling that people were doing special things for you behind the scenes, based on what they knew about you, even if they really weren't.

Like many other department stores, Marshall Field's has gone the way of the dodo bird. The company became an acquisitions target and was passed around a succession of corporate parents, starting with BATUS, then moving on to Dayton-Hudson (Target), May Company, and finally, Federated (Macy's), which retired the Marshall Field's name in 2006. My parents still mourn the day that Marshall Field's disappeared.

I'm reminded of something naturalist David Attenborough said in his film *A Life on Our Planet*. During the course of the film, Attenborough reflected on his long life while weaving into those reflections the storyline of the catastrophic loss of the earth's wild places and biodiversity. According to Attenborough, in 1937, when he was just 11 years old, the world was 66 percent untouched wilderness. As he began his career, Attenborough went to places that no one had ever been to before, saw plants and animals that no one had ever seen before, and met indigenous people who no outsider had ever met before.

As his career progressed, the earth's wilderness continued to shrink—taken by humans to exploit resources, convert forests into farms, and build thriving cities. The pace of change continued to accelerate. By 1997, the earth's wilderness had been reduced to 46 percent, and in 2020, just 37 percent of the planet's surface was wilderness. We've reached a tipping point where the pace of change will continue to accelerate, and we can expect much of the earth's wilderness to eventually disappear.

It's much the same in today's world of commerce. The kind of human shopping experiences that my dad and I enjoyed together at stores like Marshall Field's are rapidly becoming extinct. And with this loss, we are also losing something else: the human connection that we as people have always valued and longed for. In its place are digital buying experiences that in many cases undermine the connection to the customer—treating them as data, faceless, soulless financial transactions instead of as people with real needs, desires, and wants. Or bombarding them with ads for things that have no relevance to their current context. Or worse, when they finally have bought something but have a problem, pushing them into endless layers of customer service phone trees, mindless chatbots, or poorly constructed self-service FAQs.

This change is predictable, and in many ways necessary to scale, but the unintended march toward human ambivalence has pushed the customer, employee, and citizen further away than ever. I often ask a fundamental question of senior executives to test this theory. In light of all the technology, digital channels, and flood of data being collected today, what three things can they tell me about their most valuable customers that their competitors don't know? We'll circle back to this question later in this book.

Over the past 100 years, businesses have naturally evolved and become ever larger and more complex. To grow, CEOs put the emphasis on two levers in particular: driving efficiencies and productivity (controlling costs) and boosting short-term results by bombarding customers with every promotion they can think of as frequently as possible. But this is the law of diminishing marketing returns at work in full force, and the success of the latter is often left to hapless CMOs who are blamed when the expected results fail to materialize. As a result of these initiatives, the human touch has played a decreasingly important role in business—the "people" element has in fact been subordinated to the constant drive to scale.

I believe that we have taken this drive to scale too far, relying far too much on an ever-increasing arsenal of technology and gatekeepers to make up for the lack of "soul" in our interactions with customer and employees. We have neglected the human connection as we use digital to perform many of the tasks that people traditionally performed (and indeed still perform better).

Which brings us to the question: Why should we care?

We should care because our customers are telling us that they aren't happy with the status quo. We should care because we are spending more and more on technology and data, and getting less and less in return. We should care because our customers and employees are telling us that they no longer trust us. We should care because we have distanced ourselves from the real and ever-changing human signals that tell us our customers and employees feel they no longer matter. We should also care because the next big growth wave for businesses will be based on figuring out how to build purpose-driven experiences that will help those organizations that "get it" gain a lasting competitive advantage in their respective marketplaces.

We should care because building data-driven relevant and contextual experiences is where the future is going, whether or not we get on board.

Mark Curtis is head of innovation and thought leadership at Accenture Song. We discussed why people increasingly feel they no longer matter. Says Mark:

We spend a great bit of our time talking about how we can be relevant to our clients. If we're doing our job well, we spend even more time talking about how we can make our clients relevant to their customers. What we never talk about, however, is how we can make those customers feel relevant. So, my proposition here is we are looking at relevance through the wrong end of the telescope.

If we were to be truly customer focused, we would be looking at relevance from the point of view of the customer, as in how do we help make them feel relevant? In fact, if you just want to be commercial about it, I think there's a huge amount of money to be made by creating relevance engines for people.

I believe the world is in a crisis of relevance—people are suffering a decline in personal relevance, that they don't matter. And I think that's been going on for some time. There are a variety of causes for that, including the future of work which involves automation, robots, and artificial intelligence. People are worried that the skills they bring to work aren't going to be needed at some state in the near future, which makes them feel less relevant—like they no longer matter.

I agree with Mark. We need to find ways to help customers and employees feel more relevant—that they matter. In many ways, I think the world today is coming full circle. It's back to the future in the sense that what we've always valued and longed for are human connection and to feel we matter, and customers are telling us that's what they want. Few organizations of any scale can have the same level of connection that start-ups or small businesses have, so they have increasingly looked to technology to fill the void. But I believe that void cannot be filled by technology in its current form.

To be effective, data, technology, and emotional human connection need to come together to make a difference. How do we surprise, delight, and build lasting trust that can drive the next wave of growth? How do we provide the appropriate "digital kisses on the cheek" in an authentic way that makes our customers and employees feel they truly matter, something that makes our digital experiences feel as meaningful as our face-to-face experiences? Ten or 15 years ago, we couldn't do that sort of thing—we couldn't reinject humanity into all the scaled digital capabilities we've created.

But now we can.

Maybe for the first time, we now have the ability to dial back the clock and incorporate some of the genuine human experiences that we used to take for granted into digital to drive the next major wave of growth. We can accomplish this by recalibrating the power balance between customers, employees, and executive leadership—and between strategy, marketing, operations, sales, and technology—removing the labels and creating a revolutionary blur that will define these relationships for the next decade and beyond.

Ultimately, that's what this book is all about.

Some companies seem to be going in the right direction, while others aren't. The good news is that it's possible to follow some simple but powerful principles that will enable anyone to focus more on people first, but in a way that is not cost prohibitive or detrimental to the organization.

And, truth be told, it's more important than ever to apply this thinking to the enterprise to ensure that we use these technologies, data, and capabilities for good. Your business depends on it.

2

The Human Touch: ~~Customer,~~ ~~Employee, Client,~~ ~~Shareholder~~ . . . Just People

Being heard is so close to being loved that for the average person, they are almost indistinguishable.

—David Augsburger

When I first got into social media—before it was called "social media," somewhere between Friendster and Myspace—I had an epiphany about the impact digital might eventually have on our world. In 2007, I made the move from comScore to Sears Holdings, and I was tasked with building a loyalty community for Sears at a time when they had just started doing e-commerce right. They were in full turnaround mode and were running fast to catch up in ecommerce.

By all accounts, Sears could have been—should have been—as successful as Amazon, perhaps even more so. In 2000, Amazon's total revenue was about $2.8 billion.[1] That same year, Sears's revenue was $40.9 billion.[2] What ultimately turned the tide in Amazon's favor was that Sears's leadership at the time was justifiably concerned that pushing the company into online sales would hurt its 3,000 bricks-and-mortar stores scattered across the United States. So, while Sears had an online presence

(Sears.com), it was not a top priority for the company. The top priority was defending the status quo. Thus, they missed boat in e-commerce as Amazon continued to grow—and grow.

Soon after I arrived at Sears, I started thinking about what we could do to improve our digital initiatives. My first order of business was to build a little community of some of our most valuable customers and then find out more about them. Did they still like Sears? Did they still value what it stood for? Did they even *know* what it stood for? My initiative would be a challenge—I was by myself at first, I didn't have any budget for what I wanted to do, and I wasn't even sure what that should be.

Perched on some packing boxes in a small vestibule, the company literally built an office around me. I remember the construction workers asking me how many ceiling tiles were allocated to me. I had no idea what that meant or how many had been allocated, but apparently that was important for people to know. The number of tiles indicated the amount of real estate you could occupy, and accordingly your status. At the time, it seemed to me that I had been granted way too many given my bootstrapping approach.

At first, I coded a simple community platform myself—there wasn't a lot available off the shelf at the time. We weren't even using Twitter or Facebook yet. I even incorporated Survey Monkey into the platform so we could communicate with people (and because I had no budget for formal research). It wasn't pretty, but it got the job done. Every few days, I would create a little survey in Survey Monkey and send it out to all the people who were on a list of our most valuable customers—supplied to me by Research—and then I'd wait for responses. I usually sent them out on a Thursday night, and I would start getting responses the next day. People were always really good about returning those surveys.

I went through several cycles of this, and I routinely received about 1,200 responses each time. People were definitely engaged. I was about to go home late one Friday, and one of the people

I had sent the survey to responded on the public forum side of our platform. We didn't have a character limit and you could write anything you wanted. This guy wrote what I would equate to the introduction to *War and Peace* (I hadn't thought about a 140-character cap). It had bullets and exclamation points and lots and lots of words. At the very end, however, he said something that caught my attention: "Here's the story. Thank you for spending time talking to us 'loyal customers,' but as a former 'loyal customer,' I am never going to buy anything from you again."

And he just left it at that.

It was late, I was tired, and I wanted to go home. In addition, I had been having a bad week in my half-built office and was questioning whether this job was the right path for me. But I thought to myself, "If I believe what I believe, I should probably respond to this guy and see what's going on."

I wrote back, "Sorry to hear that. What went wrong?"

The man quickly responded: "Here's the thing. I have been a loyal customer of Sears, particularly the Craftsman side of Sears, for many years." Our Craftsman tool customers were ultra-committed to the company. The tools were and are high quality, and the brand promise was a 100 percent satisfaction guarantee—if something went wrong with any Craftsman product, we would replace it no questions asked with no time limit.

The former customer continued, "Every year I bought thousands of dollars' worth of Craftsman tools—you should be able to see that. One time I bought a little vise-grip at Sears that was not a Craftsman tool and only had a one-year warranty. But, wouldn't you know it, a year to the date after I bought the vise-grip it snapped in half. I didn't think that you were going to replace it per se. But I'm a 15-year loyalist, I buy thousands of dollars' worth of merchandise from Sears each year, surely there was something you could do to help me."

Apparently, when he went back to the store, the salesperson told him he could just buy a new one for $40. He didn't like that answer so he talked to the manager. The manager said, "Sorry, I can't do anything—it's only warrantied for a year and your broken tool is outside that." He escalated his problem up the chain. He wrote letters to corporate. No one responded.

He told me, "Basically, the message you gave me is that nobody knew who I was. Nobody knew how much I had bought. Nobody knew how loyal I was. And, nobody thought that it was worth spending much time helping with this problem. So, I decided to stop buying from Sears. I took my Sears credit card out of my wallet, I put it somewhere in my desk, and I forgot about it. I just wanted you to know that."

So, in for a penny, in for a pound. I responded, "I don't know if I can help, but let me see what I can do." This was a commitment I had no way of knowing for sure if I could keep.

In desperation I reached out to a colleague of mine who was in the Special Care Division that had just been spun up. "I don't know if you can do anything about this," I said, "but this doesn't seem right."

I should have checked back that weekend because, by the time I got back to the office on Monday, there was a sequel to *War and Peace* waiting for me. I thought, "Oh my God, I made this even worse."

There again were three big paragraphs with numbers on them. The guy said, "I just wanted to get back to you and let you know what happened. First, I didn't really expect you to get back to me. I was literally just blowing off steam." He went on for a while before getting to his second point.

"Second," he continued, "I don't know what you thought you could do, but in my mind there was nothing you could do because I had already given up on the relationship. I was never going to buy anything from you again. It was nice that you thought you could try, but at the end of the day, you weren't going to move my opinion about this. You guys just didn't care and that was the message that came across."

I felt a wave of relief. It looked like I hadn't made this person's situation better, but at least I hadn't made it worse.

He went on to his third point: "I don't know what you actually did, but your colleague reached out to me on Saturday, and she was the nicest person I ever met. She gave me the nicest apology I've ever had. My wife doesn't even apologize to me like that after arguments. She gave me a gift card for $40, but most important, that apology meant the world to me."

And then he wrote at the bottom of his message, "So I just want to let you know that today I found that Sears card I threw in the bottom of my desk drawer. I put it back in my wallet."

"Okay, what does this all mean?" I wondered.

An Epiphany

Maybe I was lucky with this Sears loyalist, or maybe I just proved that it's worth talking to your customers. But I decided what it boiled down to was that, as human beings, what we're really striving for in all our interactions—whether they're digital or face-to-face, whether they're personal or public—is to feel that we matter. And if brands, companies, nonprofits, governments, and so on can understand that, focus again on the people side of the equation, and make customers and employees feel like they matter in all their interactions, they'll win.

Ask yourself the fundamental empathy-led question: How would I feel if I were in their shoes?

This is the thing that will make the difference between organizations that succeed in the twenty-first century and those that don't. Digital is important because it helps you scale, but it's not the technology on its own that makes the difference. It's how you *humanize* digital, and it's also how you humanize *human*.

Accenture has done lots of research into what we call the *World of Experience*. Here are some of the key findings:

- 64 percent of people think that customer experience is more important than price—price is no longer the reliable game changer it used to be.
- 89 percent of customers stop doing business with a brand following a poor customer experience—humanizing digital for better interactions can lower the risk of attrition.
- 65 percent of companies say improving their data analysis is important for customer experience, but currently, recommendations and predictions often do not provide enough context to deliver an understanding of customer needs, motivations, and frustrations.
- 5 percent of brands claim to have a seamless customer experience, indicating that too many marketers are hyperfocused on efficiency and market reach.
- 54 percent of brands currently deliver experiences that result in cart abandonment.
- 73 percent of marketers have less than half of their channels connected, leading to silos and limited learning.

The World of Experience has fundamentally changed.[3] To stay relevant today and into the future, companies must evolve—keeping a step ahead of change that is all around us. They must quickly adapt to differentiate in a world where brands are being experienced in new ways. The year of COVID—2020—was a year like no other, a year in which change washed over us even faster than before, shifting the digital world. Instead of just products, services, or brands, consumers want experiences. As a result, companies must provide experiences that are responsive to the individual human needs of customers.

Digital, using the tremendous power of data analytics, is core to these efforts.

But to be most effective, it must be a combination of digital *and* human. The complexity of products requires humans to be a key part of sales and marketing. Digital must embrace and augment the human players involved throughout the process, and it must do this empathetically—focusing on customer needs first and foremost.

Marketers and their brands have come to a crossroads in how they do business. Before 2020, companies focused on leveraging the tremendous power of data and analytics. Unfortunately, this was often at the expense of the human dimension.

Today, it's clear that people are yearning to be able to trust, and they want it more than ever. They expect personalized experiences, built on real-time contextualization of their preferences. But they want each interaction to connect with them on a human level so they can come away from those experiences feeling they have been heard, their needs have been addressed, and above all, they matter.

The ability to meet this expectation will be a key determinant in the growth and sustainability of every organization.

Of *your* organization.

What Makes Humans Human?

One of my favorite authors is Desmond Morris. He earned his doctorate in animal behavior at Oxford and served for a time as curator of mammals at the London Zoo. He wrote a slew of amazing books, but the one that got people really talking was *The Naked Ape*, published in 1967. The book looks at people—their behavior and morphology—in the context of other primates. I love Morris's work because, as a historian, as a sociologist, if you don't study these things, you'll miss them.

Why are things the way they are? Why do we humans behave the way we do? Why do we come together? Why are we even *able* to come together? What are the traits that make us uniquely human? Through behavioral observation of other animals, Morris was able to apply everything he learned to humans. He could see these interactions between humans—shared with and evolved from our animal ancestors—every day, doing whatever they were doing. And he explains them in a very convincing way.

We humans are who we are because of evolution and natural selection. Behaviors that helped someone reproduce and perpetuate their DNA were selected for. Behaviors that worked against someone's being able to reproduce and perpetuate their DNA were eventually extinguished. Morris said that one of the main reasons we can coexist as a species is that, when we came together, it made natural sense. But very quickly we learned that we needed to have some rules. Otherwise, people would take advantage of one another, which would destroy trust and be a disincentive to working together for the overall good of the species.

The Vikings have long been painted as a fearsome clan of Norse invaders who destroyed everyone and everything in their path. The historian J.M. Wallace-Hadrill—who always had an interesting turn of phrase at the ready—explained that most people considered Vikings to basically be the Dark Age equivalent of "groups of long-haired tourists who occasionally roughed up the natives."[4] But as Wallace-Hadrill pointed out, the Viking culture was just as sophisticated, if not more sophisticated, than the "advanced" cultures they conquered. They just had bad PR.

That's the same sort of lens we should put on business. I think we take things for granted because there are those for whom it's in their interest to paint them in that light. And the result is you don't do anything—you miss the opportunity. You're always asking those perennial questions, such as, "How do we get more innovative?" "How do we beat Amazon?" "How can we be like Uber?" It's kind of like the millionaire question: How do you make a million dollars? Well, first you go get a million dollars. It's the same with data. "Why, a four-year-old child could understand this report!" Groucho Marx once remarked. "Run out and find me a four-year-old child. I can't make head nor tail out of it."

The answers to the perennial questions, such as those just mentioned are almost that obvious. You've got to make a commitment to be an innovative organization. And it must be top-down, bottom-up. And you've got to completely divorce yourself from the thought that, because you do things differently, because things don't go well, and because there are failures, you would abandon that tack. Holding onto doing things differently is the whole point. That's why, for every Amazon, there were probably a thousand other start-ups that didn't survive.

And luck has a lot to do with it—*human* luck. That concept has a lot to do with how we've progressed. It's being willing to take risks when we can't even see the return. We just feel it. That is a unique thing, and you can't get that into a computer program easily.

We want to be able to play it safe and dissect everything and then figure out what went right with Amazon. And then, if we do those things that Amazon did right—we put all those things together and stir the pot—we think we can be just as successful as they are. The reality is, of course, no, because Amazon is the result of many decisions that were made over a long period of time—some right, some wrong. Jeff Bezos had an almost religious-like intent, which was "I believe I'm right. I'm going to go all-in right or wrong."

And Bezos could have been very wrong. In fact, for years, everybody said he was wrong. Amazon was growing but there was no profit. And according to the conventional wisdom at the time, if your company didn't generate profits, it was surely on the road to bankruptcy. No profit no business. But Bezos proved them wrong. Building market share and revenue came first, then the profits eventually followed. And if he had listened to all those people who said he was wrong, there might not be an Amazon today.

There were two important lessons I believe enhanced Amazon's luck beyond technology and a solid supply chain. The realization that people needed a lot of help finding things to reduce wasted time, and they also wanted recommendations from other trustworthy people before they bought something—two very human needs.

The point is, how do you get back to taking advantage of the things that make us most human? And that's how you human-ize relationships with customers. That's how you humanize the innovation process. That's how you humanize the use of data. It's empathetic, it's emotional, and sometimes it's just intuited. It's not always about math and purity of the algorithm. Math and algorithms can help for sure, but creativity and the connec-tions it can create is something that makes us uniquely human, and it is very hard for a machine to be creative—at least so far in our history.

Tomorrow's right around the corner, and I suspect it will be a very different place.

A Frustrating Example

I have two young children, both girls, and when our oldest was going to turn five, we wanted to get her something special to celebrate. The only thing we could think of was a bicycle. When I was a kid, my dad would have gone to the Marshall Field's department store and there would have been an entire bicycle section in the toy department. The salesperson would explain the pros and cons of the different bicycles and my dad could try them out right there. Once he decided on the one he wanted, my dad would pay for it, stick it in the trunk of our car, and drive it home. The entire process was sometimes fraught with absence of choice, or high-pressure salesmanship, but it was simple and relatively straightforward.

Today, you feel like you're more on your own, and in many ways you are on your own—spoiled for choice but no better able to trust. When we decided to buy our daughter that bike for her fifth birthday, I had to first do some research. I did a Google search for reviews and lists of the best bikes for kids. I became conversant with different features—things like knobby versus street tires, braking systems, and internally geared hubs. I learned a great deal about the advantages and disadvantages of lighter and heavier bikes and different frame sizes. This was a good part of the process.

The process was a *lot* different from the one my dad went through when he walked into the Marshall Field's department store in downtown Chicago and was advised by a salesperson who was good at his job, knew a lot about bikes, and who saw my dad as a person—a friend and a father who wanted to show his love for a son and revisit a bit of the feeling he himself had when got his first bike.

After doing my due diligence, I narrowed down the choices to a few different bikes, and I logged on to Amazon to check pricing and availability and read the reviews. Eventually, I found a bike that checked all the boxes for me—it looked really nice, it was the right price, and it had great reviews. The final box to be checked was delivery—our daughter's birthday was about five weeks out, but I needed time to assemble the bike and hide it at her grandparents' house. According to Amazon, the bike would be delivered in just a couple days, so that sealed the deal.

Plenty of time I thought, so I bought it.

Unfortunately, the bike purchase didn't take long to go off the rails.

The promised delivery date of a couple days turned into a week, and then the week turned into two. I received an email from Amazon notifying me that, even though the bike was in stock, it was running behind. Two weeks stretched to three and a half. The problem was that it was now just a little more than a week to go before my daughter's birthday, and I needed the bike. It still hadn't arrived, and there was no certainty when it would. It was time to get hold of someone at Amazon and find out when the bike was really going to arrive. But that turned out to be easier said than done.

I'm pretty digitally savvy—I know where look and what rocks to turn over when it comes to finding customer service people. But in the case of Amazon, it was ultrahard to find a real person I could escalate to and ask, "What's going on here—what can you do to get me the bike in time for my daughter's birthday?" I was getting increasingly frustrated with my dilemma. I discovered that Amazon's digital experience is great, at least until something goes wrong with your order.

Another day went by, and I was down to four days before my daughter's birthday. At that point, I was convinced the bike was not going to show up—it probably wasn't in the warehouse, and it might not exist at all. We did a little back and forth and the Amazon customer service rep told me via email, "We'll contact the seller and figure out what's going on. It should be with you."

I was getting ultrafrustrated by this point—my emails weren't doing the trick, so it was time to get on the phone with someone and find out if the bike was on the way or if I needed to scour Chicago to find one.

Persistence paid off though. After four or five attempts I got through to a live person. I was trying to keep myself calm but it wasn't easy. Knowing how difficult a service rep's life can be, I reined in my emotions and started with, "I know it's not your fault, but I'm having a really tough time here. I feel like I'm getting the runaround and I just need a straight answer. If the answer is that the bike is not available and I need to go and do something else, that's fine—I'll just cancel the whole thing. And if the answer is 'We found it and we can get it to you in time,' fantastic. I need to know one way or the other, right now."

I don't know if Amazon has changed its ordering system, but at the time they weren't geared toward making complex alterations after the fact. The rep had to come up with a creative workaround that I'm certain most of his colleagues wouldn't have known how to do.

"I'm going to create this sort of duplicate website over here," he told me. "You're going to first cancel your order, then you're going to go to the link that I will send you. You're going to select the same thing. I will give you a credit on everything, including the delivery charge. And you will select this because I found the bike in stock, and I confirmed that we'll get it to you within two days. Then you have to go ahead and make that purchase. I'm going to give you a credit for the cost of delivery because you've been a great customer and this is really bad service."

And it worked. But it took an empowered and highly knowledgeable human to help me. Amazon's ordering system couldn't do it, as amazing as it might be. The experience actually made me feel better about Amazon because of this living, breathing service rep who was willing to be a little creative. The fact that he took the time to listen (and most important, emphasize like that salesperson back in Marshall Field's) to me was a big deal.

One more thing from the consumer perspective: let me know that you've at least gone the extra mile. If the bike turned out not to be available, the rep could have said, "I can't find it. I'm sorry, but I'm going to give you a credit. By the way, I was able to just quickly look online and there are some bikes just like this in stock at the Walmart down the road from you." That makes a difference—it leaves an impression. We remember and long for the Miracle on 34th Street every holiday season and then seemingly go back to internecine warfare for the rest of the year, with every battle being a zero-sum game. It doesn't need to be that way.

I thought, what if you could productize that? How can we make things better—more human for people generally—not just, how do we sell them more shoes or bikes or whatever? How do we make people feel like they did a good thing and they weren't exhausted at the end of it? That would make a very real difference in their experience with digital. That would be more empathetic, more human.

A Bridge Too Far?

But, as we all know, the online world is not all good. Increasingly, digital is a double-edged sword and sometimes technology gets it terribly wrong. For example, it can be much more invasive and frustrating than it should be.

In a *New York Times* article, author Charles Duhigg told the story about how retailing giant Target decided to analyze shopper cue-routine-reward loops—neurological loops at the core of every habit—and then use the insights gained to market the company's products more effectively. According to Duhigg, some questions came up as part of a marketing discussion: Would it be possible to use data to anticipate a customer need, before other retailers? And if so, would it be possible to tell if a customer is pregnant?[5]

It's not hard to imagine why any retailer would want to be able to figure this out. Think of all the things new parents—and prospective new parents—buy during the course of a pregnancy and the birth of a child. There are cribs and crib mattresses; sheets and blankets; bibs and burp cloths; breast pumps, bottles, and formula; changing pads and diapers (*lots* of diapers); onesies and undershirts and pants and socks and booties; diaper wipes and other cleaning supplies; maternity clothing and prenatal vitamins; books and toys—the list goes on and on. Being able to identify such customers would enable an organization to better target shoppers with highly focused product offers.

Allegedly, a team went to work on the problem, and after combing through and analyzing a treasure trove of marketing data, they were able to develop a prediction score based on 25 specific products that, when purchased, indicated a customer was likely to be pregnant. What's more, they were able to fairly accurately predict a customer's actual due date based on their buying habits, and to allow changes to marketing offers depending on the stage of the pregnancy or the birth of a child. Seemingly, this would be a win-win for the customer and the business.

One can imagine that in this day and age, any and all organizations understand the value of customer data and passionately pursue the Holy Grail of marketing—anticipating a customer's needs before they even realize those needs themselves. However, the real question shouldn't just be, "*Can* we do something?" The first question should be "*Should* we do something?" We should base that on the exploration of a fundamental question: "As customers, how would this make *us* feel?" This is something the most empathetic of we humans would process in a nanosecond, and overlooking that question can lead to unintended consequences for sure.

According to Duhigg, approximately one year after this model was implemented, an angry man stomped into a local Minneapolis-area Target store, asking for the manager. "My daughter got this in the mail!" the man heatedly explained to the manager. "She's still in high school, and you're sending her coupons for baby clothes and cribs? Are you trying to encourage her to get pregnant?"[6]

The manager looked at the coupons the man held in his hand, and they included offers for maternity clothing and nursery furniture. The envelope the coupons were mailed in was indeed addressed to the young daughter of this angry man. All the manager could do was apologize for this obvious mistake, which he did profusely.

A few days later, says Duhigg, it was the father's turn to apologize. He called the manager and said, "I had a talk with my daughter. It turns out there's been some activities in my house I haven't been completely aware of. She's due in August. I owe you an apology."[7]

While there remain questions about the details of this story, it is nonetheless a good parable that should make us stop and think. It's one thing for a marketer to be able to anticipate something a customer might do, but it's another thing altogether to overreach and miss the context. When my boss, Glen Hartman, and I talk about the importance of contextual experience in situations like this, the hardest thing is discerning the moment that matters most to a customer and directing them to the right thing—changing their experience as a result.

The Digital Dilemma—Meeting Needs Versus Surprise and Delight

Despite the bad experiences we all have had with online purchases and other transactions, where digital gets it right is the promise of being able to do things that we couldn't even imagine a few years ago. In just one example, today we can find things to buy online that we've never been able to find before. I started using Etsy for the very first time a couple years ago and I was blown away by the experience.

Etsy has really thought through the typical ups and downs customers often have when they're dealing with solo vendors or small business owners. And Etsy also gives customers access to unique items that people from every corner of the earth have personally made. When I placed an order and the package arrived from Bratislava, I would never have imagined that's where the item came from. Being able to use technology in this way, with just a few clicks, is amazing and it's having a remarkably positive impact on humanity. It gives individuals tremendous reach and real power.

But context is everything.

As Glen Hartman, Global Commerce Lead of Accenture Song, illustrates in this example:

> *Let's say you have a big family, and you do grocery shopping for your family every Saturday. Your grocery store happens to be doing everything they possibly can do in the advanced world of technology and data and experience, and they're doing a great job—they've got it all nailed. Most grocery stores don't, but yours does.*

You love this store—you're a member of their loyalty program and you have their app on your phone. You like to load your shopping list into the app, and when you set foot into the store, they know you're there because they're using location data from your phone.

The second you walk into the store, and once you think about it, they're going to work with you on their most important outcomes and metrics. There are three metrics they care most about. One is to get more customer trips into the store. Two, when customers are in the store, they want them to buy certain types of merchandise—usually things the CPG [consumer packaged goods] *companies are pushing for inventory reasons. They usually display this merchandise on endcaps and in other prominent locations. The third metric is the cart—buy more. Now, this could apply to online or offline commerce, it doesn't matter—the concept is the same.*

So, you walk into your favorite grocery store on Saturday, and they've got everything right. They see you there, they see your shopping list, they start serving up coupons tailored to your list, and they want to make sure you're going to buy some of the products on the endcaps. They know what you like—you've been to some of the cooking classes they run, and they know you love to cook.

They look at the shopping list on your phone, and instead of looking at it just as a shopping list, they look at it as a set of ingredients. Suddenly, they send you a message via the app, "If you add these two other products, you can make this great recipe tonight." They even serve you a video showing how to make the recipe and a coupon to get those two other products at a discount. Now they're cross selling and upselling—they're making the cart bigger.

You're loving it—it speaks to you, it's personalized, it's relevant. It's all good.

Then one day you show up at that same grocery store, but it's not on your usual Saturday. It's 11 o'clock on a Tuesday morning. It turned out that one of your children was sick and you had to go pull her out of school, take her to the doctor, and get a prescription. You've got to get back to work for a presentation at 1 o'clock and you can't be late. You went to the grocery store to get your prescription filled—they have a pharmacy in the back, and the doctor already sent the prescription to the pharmacy electronically—and you need to buy a vaporizer, Vicks VapoRub, and some juice and cough drops. That's it—you need to get in and out as fast as you can.

When you walk into the store, you don't want coupons. You don't want recipes. You don't want any of that. You just want to get the things on your shopping list and go. The company can see what's on your shopping list and it thinks, "Something's up with Pete—it looks like he's in a hurry. Why don't I take the things on his list, and I'll heatmap the store to show him where everything is so he can get in and out quicker?" Or, better than that, you're met at the front of the store by a concierge who says, "I noticed these things are on your list, so I already gathered them for you, including the prescription. Here you go. Since you're in our reward system, we have your payment information, and we'll just charge it to your account—you don't need to check out. Don't worry, go take care of your kid. I hope everything is all right."

In that moment, the grocery store broke every single rule they have for a success metric. They didn't get you into the store, you didn't buy products from the endcaps, and you didn't spend more. Those are failures on every level for the way they manage their business. But in the moment, because they've read your intent—you were in a very different situation that Tuesday morning than you are on a typical Saturday—it's a huge win for you the customer, and a wonderful, much more relevant experience of personalization that serves your goals.

That kind of experience would be a game changer—a remarkable application of the power and promise of digital, but we're not there yet. The good news is we're getting closer, it's not all that far away. The technology is there.

Creating Moments That Matter

We were recently doing some brainstorming around creating moments that matter in financial services and retail banking—looking for ways to humanize the process. If you have ever bought a house and applied for a mortgage (particularly post 2008), then you've experienced being asked to lay bare your *entire* personal financial situation—embarrassing bits and all.

First there's the obligatory credit check to assess how much debt you have, what kind of debt it is, and how reliable you are at paying it off. Have you ever declared bankruptcy or skipped credit card, car loan, or other consumer debt payments? Obviously, that'll show up in your credit report. You'll need to provide your personal income tax filings and W-2 forms, any real estate taxes paid for at least the past couple of years, plus assessments, investment statements for you and your spouse or partner, and, if you own a business, you may have to provide those income tax filings and a detailed profit-and-loss statement too. You'll of course need to provide copies of recent paystubs to corroborate your claimed income along with bank statements that show you actually have the down payment funds available to you to complete the home purchase.

I'll wager your parents never even knew this much about you. Truth be told, you might not have known this much about you either.

When you complete the mortgage loan application and approval process, there's probably no institution on the planet that knows more about you, at least financially, than the organization that originates your loan. Maybe 99.9 percent of the time, that's where it begins and ends. The mortgage lender knows what you own, what you're buying, how much cash and other assets you possess, how many lines of credit you have, what kinds and amounts of debt you carry, and on and on. They have all this information, but in most cases not much is done with it. Of course, there may be regulatory issues that constrain a bank from sharing that financial information with other parts of the organization or outside its own four walls, but this data is tremendously valuable to marketers.

If would be the perfect time, even if you couldn't do a very sophisticated handoff of every piece of data, to do some sort of magic around it and understand exactly what the customer's next move is going to be. For example, they're probably going to need to insure their new home, so maybe it's time for them to think about changing insurance companies or changing products.

They're probably going to decorate or renovate their home, especially if they plan to live in it themselves and not rent it out. So, they're going to buy a lot more things for their home in the next few months. If I notice they're running up their credit cards at West Elm or Crate and Barrel, I could offer them a low-cost loan to transfer the high-interest-rate credit card balances.

The possibilities are virtually endless. And that's just the financial side of it. But often what happens is nothing, or at best a slew of product and service offers divorced from any understanding of who you are, what you might really need, or where you are in moment that matters to you most.

Whether we idealize it or not, 30, 40, 50 years ago, our parents likely personally knew their bank manager, or if they lived in a small town with just one bank, the president. They would have had to at least talk with that person before they were approved for a loan. It was like a scene out of *It's a Wonderful Life* with Jimmy Stewart playing the role of small-town banker George Bailey and all the lives that were touched and made better with his help.

When this kind of banking worked at its best, you had a relationship with someone who knew you and knew your family and knew you were good for it. They were empathetic to your needs. They were human, and they treated you in a human way. At its worst, you might have found yourself with Henry Potter—a caricature of an extremely unforgiving banker (and a not-so-subtle indictment of runaway capitalism). But in truth, which character do you feel you are more likely to encounter? And have institutions done enough to build trust beyond agreeing to keep your money safe?

When I was getting ready to go to college in the UK, I opened a bank account at Citibank. And even though I wasn't making much money for Citibank at the time, the bank was there for me when I needed their help. When I had to find someone who would write a letter of introduction so I could get a visa, the manager of my family's branch wrote one for me—on Citibank letterhead. The letter said something along the lines of, "Robert's parents are great.

They've been banking with us X number of years, and I can recommend them highly." No doubt, the level of personal attention from a big bank—from most banks and financial institutions—has disappeared. Even as our fortunes have increased, that high level of humanity, empathy, and intimacy we used to routinely enjoy seems to be, at least on the surface, a rare if not exotic commodity.

It's not that you expect a bank to keep that infrastructure the same as it was 50 years ago—it can't and it shouldn't. But that bank could be making a lot of the things it does a lot easier for customers, much more proactive, much more thoughtful—more human. I applied for a mortgage refinance over a year ago, and in the middle of the process—which took many more weeks than anticipated—I was still getting invitations from the marketing department extoling the benefits of refinancing.

Why?

Did they not know I was already a customer, in process to refinance? One can argue at length about whether companies are people, but they are composed of people. And those humans have all been there; they all know what they like and what they dislike.

As one of my colleagues and I started to break it down, we decided that there are two levels. One level represents tactical moments that matter—things that if you just eliminated them or made them easier, that would win you a lot of points with your customers. Like reordering a checkbook (if any of us use those much anymore), or making it easy to initiate a loan application without asking for the same information twice, or simply giving customers more control over the alerts and reminders they receive on their account. However, enough of this exists today that's still bad that it colors relationships between brands and their customers.

The other level includes the more strategic moments that matter. This could include zeroing in on the individual goals that people have and realizing that they're not really interested in wealth management goals, but instead in their life goals. So, what if banks were more like life coaches? Instead of looking at a customer's life as a linear game to retirement, they could take the 50,000-foot view of what they want to accomplish along the way.

They might tell a client, "You want to travel every five years with your family—let's figure out what that looks like." They might want to take a sabbatical every 10 years, or start a business, or go back to school. The bank could do something different by making the relationship and the products offered to customers specifically relevant to them and what they want to do with their lives. Even if customers' goals change, the bank will change with them. And here is the important point to keep in mind: in order to do that well, institutions need to be able to listen, synthesize, and act. That is what builds trust and loyalty.

I think the old way of selling to financial customers, the "Yes, we have this fantastic team of wealth managers who will take your rollover money and use Monte Carlo simulations to outperform Wall Street," is in need of a significant overhaul. The framework of community first is key to that.

When I first started to build communities, we thought really hard about how we could engage with customers in ways that made them feel like they mattered (to us, and most important, to one another). One of the first retail communities I built attracted around a million and a half people within about 18 months. But what was more important about it than just the sheer number of people was that a percentage of them were *extremely* engaged in the community.

We certainly gathered and analyzed data, but when we looked at that data, we found something interesting we hadn't seen before: data that existed in no other database. We discovered that the more we actually engaged, asked questions, answered questions, shared and listened to ideas, the more popular the community became and the more participants were willing to tell us about themselves.

We created a real community of fans hanging out with other likeminded people. We allowed that community to engage with each other and to grow organically. During the second year after we initiated the community, we encouraged people to write reviews. In fact, we expanded the loyalty program to include rewarding people with points for content they wrote good or bad, such as reviews—just because they helped others.

I remember it was just after Thanksgiving that second year when we discovered there was a whole group of mothers who spontaneously got together on our platform the weekend before Black Monday. They had what they dubbed a "Black Monday virtual sleepover," where they talked about what they were going to buy for their kids, the good deals, the not-so-good deals, places they could find things they wanted, and much more. We didn't interfere with what they were doing—we just watched from the sidelines.

They were being as human as you can be, doing the things that humans enjoy doing. Talking, sharing, providing others with the benefit of their knowledge, having fun, enjoying being part of a community. And they were doing it in a digital environment that facilitated their interaction, and above all, trust.

David Kidder is co-founder and CEO of Bionic, part of Accenture Song. He reminds us of the importance of seeing customers above all else as people and remembering that we're in business to serve them, not them to serve us. Says David:

> We have the idea of customers—that is us selling to people for them. We need to move from for to with, we need to move from customers to people, and we need to move our mindset from a total addressable marketplace role—which is zero sum, doing it to win—to total addressable problems and needs of the world.
>
> The question is, are we doing that? Do we see the people? Are we doing it with them? Are we doing this in the needs? Those core ideas are almost the opposite of how most companies think today. And what's underneath this, their reality, is just a subset of their intentional choices. They're disconnected from that why. And what's underneath the why is only really an innate state of one or two things. That's fear versus abundance, which is why they're stuck.
>
> Why are we here? Because we've lost our North Star.

3

Putting Empathy and Expertise Back into the Equation

Empathy is about standing in someone else's shoes, feeling with his or her heart, seeing with his or her eyes.

Not only is empathy hard to outsource and automate, but it makes the world a better place.

—Daniel Pink

Creating a truly people-focused organization is ultimately all about *empathizing* with our customers and employees—walking a mile in their shoes as the old saying goes. It's taking the time and expending the effort—solo and with your team and larger organization—to actually *think* about and *experience* what it's like to be your customer.

To gather information about your complete range of products and services, to buy them, to put them to use in your daily life, and to discover what happens when things go right, and when they go wrong. It's also about power sharing—trust cannot be built unless all parties feel they are participants in the process. And guess what? This is *not* an HR function; it is something that needs to devolve to every individual. Seventy-six percent of executives in an Accenture survey said that organizations need to dramatically reengineer the experiences that matter.[1] They can do this by putting people first.

All the feedback we generate as we experience for ourselves what it's like to be our customers should be baked into the experiences we create or that we ask our technologies to deliver. Unfortunately, it is really, really hard. Most organizations that I encounter say they want to be more customer or employee centric; they want to be more agile, entrepreneurial, and innovative. They know these are qualities critical to ensuring they don't miss the next big growth wave sparked by access to technology and data. However, for all the intent, it is still pretty clear that most institutions remain locked in to processes and thinking from the last century instead of the twenty-first.

We think in terms of marketing and commerce, we think in terms of sales, we think in terms of customer care, and we think in terms of all the processes required to make these functions work. We decide who is responsible for each and how we bring those elements together as though they need to be assembled and negotiated.

But what we really need to do is erase those rigid distinctions and realign our organizations to the concept that, in this day and age, when many if not most people within an institution touch the customer in some way, we can ill afford to color within our traditional lines.

So what can we do to solve this problem—to give authentic, empathetic human experiences a more prominent role in our businesses today while building trust and driving measurable growth?

I propose the creation of a *new* operational framework—the *blur*—with the CEO taking core responsibility for orchestrating and driving a people-centric approach to the business and the experiences required to drive real trust and loyalty which in turn will drive real strategic impact.

This new breed of CEO must be able to motivate, innovate, and ask the tough questions—not only, "What is the impact to our bottom-line?" but "Are we thinking of people first in all of this?" That is, how might a decision impact a customer, employee, vendor, and owner? This, I believe, is the starting point for changing the way all the different operational organizational elements work—sales, marketing, IT, and so forth.

We keep talking about humanizing this and transforming that, and everyone gets excited about these ideas and nod their heads in support. But then we go right back to the way we have always worked, putting customer experience onto the back burner. We have to get that report done and on the boss's desk by the end of the day; we have to figure out why a customer's order didn't arrive on time. It's tyranny of the urgent, not the important.

But if you had a top-down commitment to understanding your customer, that would be transformative in most organizations today. Not from a typical, "who is your customer?" standpoint, but instead, "what is the context of those customer needs?" and "what's important in terms of building better interactions to drive better relationships?" Then having someone who can see how that customer lives, breathes, and engages gets ground down across *all* the processes—all the organizational touchpoints. That, I believe, is where it gets interesting.

Experiencing What a Customer Feels

I have done a lot of customer research during my career—hundreds of segmentations and conjoint analyses and targeting exercises—but I oddly found that the more data I had at my fingertips, the more I grew to feel that I didn't really understand the customer as well as I should. A colleague of mine once told me the best way to understand if a client really knows their customers is to ask them to take out a piece of paper and write down three things they know about their most valuable customers that their competitors don't already know. It is rare that anyone (marketer, salesperson, or C-suite executive) can truly answer that question. There is always something missing because, more often than not, we haven't walked in the shoes of an ordinary customer.

Increasingly, I've personally gotten in the habit of becoming a customer of many of my clients. For example, in early 2020—pre-COVID—we renovated a couple of our bathrooms. I decided to select my client's products and go through the same virtual design experience that any other customer would go through to see what it was like. This wasn't anything that I was paid or asked to do, and the client had no idea I had signed on to be *their* customer.

The company has physical design centers where you can view the company's products and meet with professional interior designers who at no charge will work from your ideas to create a finished design. For a relatively modest fee, however, you can instead choose the company's virtual bathroom design service, which includes several online meetings with a designer along with custom 3D renderings, a curated box of swatches and samples delivered to your home or office, and referrals to remodeling companies in your area.

The promise sounds pretty good, right?

It did to my wife and me, and we were excited to use the service.

When we had completed the design process, I gathered my notes and offered some candid feedback to my client. I even created a PowerPoint to illustrate visually all my experiences (good and bad) as a customer. I also shared some of my experiences with other companies and start-ups that also do online, virtual design for comparison.

The first realization was that to me (and most customers, I would submit) starting with design is key. People need reassurance, especially when making a complex and expensive purchase such as a kitchen or bath. Just having an option to connect with someone virtually or in person is important, and this particular experience was very hard to find.

I proceeded to explain that the design service was easier to find via a Google search than on the client's own website, and once we eventually found the service, the value proposition wasn't all that clear. It seemed like they were hiding it. Other newer virtual design offerings like Decorist, Havenly, or Modsy (all start-ups) were very clear up front about why I should use them and what to expect, so had any customer used those services, they no doubt would be expecting something similar.

And in truth, once we signed up and went through the process and received a design, the quality of the outcome was very high. It was the journey to get there that seemed disconnected from the context of our needs.

Where the start-ups got users engaged quickly and provided areas to collaborate at each step, my client was much more traditional in its approach. Instead of instantly learning about our needs and preferences and engaging in a collaborative dialogue, after we got well into the virtual design process, my wife and I had to schedule a formal design interview. Instead of developing several concepts quickly, we had to wait several weeks to receive just one, and only the designer could edit it. Instead of providing an interactive design area where we could make edits or look at different options on our own, our experience was static.

This disconnect continued through to the store as well. When we arrived, I told the salesperson who greeted us that we had started the virtual design process and asked if she could look us up in her system to at least see if some of the products were available to view.

She unfortunately couldn't find our virtual design as the systems were not connected and there was no web access in the store. But she was a trouper, and after many valiant attempts to access different systems—and about 35 or 40 minutes of waiting—the salesperson was finally able to find our virtual design order and pull up our design and list of materials. My guess is that had I had been an ordinary customer, I might not have waited those 35 or 40 minutes. But I did wait because I was curious about how this interaction with my client was going to play out.

Once we were able to pull up our order, I quickly realized it was only a flat file—she couldn't click on an item, say a faucet, and order it directly from the company. She would need to manually enter that item in another system and create an order form.

When I asked if we could do that, the very sweet, very nice woman replied, "Oh, no, you don't want to do that."

"Why not?" I asked, knowing full well that we had been hired by the client to enable and encourage direct commerce.

Now here is what was wonderful and very human: clearly wanting to look out for my best interests, the woman said, "Because you'll pay more if you buy the products directly from us online—I can't apply any discounts. You want to go through a contractor or a dealer who can."

So here's the moral of my story: As a customer willing to spend a considerable amount of money, I wanted someone who could help with a design and, more important, had the flexibility to collaborate and edit in real time; I wanted the process to challenge our thinking and provide solid options. But above all, when we were ready to buy, I wanted the process to be easy and transparent. Whether buying online, in the store, or via chat or phone, there should be one record of our design order, access to notes, and a smooth ordering process no matter who was dealing with us.

The last thing I shared with my client was something these agile start-ups included in their value proposition: if we changed our mind or thought of something else we wanted, or discovered the items we bought on discount later, they would advocate for us. That last one we didn't even need to worry about as each of the start-ups had a virtual concierge that would look for 90 days after our purchase and advocate for a refund from any of their partners without us even asking.

While my client's salesperson was very empathetic to my plight, she was essentially sabotaged by the company's existing technology, data, and processes. The power to advocate for the customer and ensure a good experience was somewhere else.

The good news is that after I relayed my story to my client, the company took action to improve its customer experience based on it. The epiphany was that the key perspective in its digital transformation was missing—the customer story was not represented up until that point.

Why is that important? We're all customers, and we have good experiences, bad experiences, and some in between. Putting yourself in the shoes of your customer is the best way to discover whether your systems are serving them well and where there are shortfalls that need to be fixed. There's really no better way to find out if your systems are designed for empathetic response than to experience them for yourself.

The Power of Empathetic Design and The Moving Truck from Hell

I have rented moving trucks many times in the past, and it's never been a big deal. More recently, the company I typically use seems to have put a lot of effort into technology to make the experience easier and more efficient for the customer, creating smartphone apps and providing better automated communication.

Of course, I personally think that's great. I can book a vehicle online or through an app, then walk into the truck pickup location, and I don't have to spend a whole bunch of time doing paperwork or taking care of other administrative trivia. But recently, when I went in to pick up a truck I had reserved online the night before, it was unfortunately not ready to go. And that was just the beginning of my experience with the moving truck from hell.

It is difficult to ensure consistency in an industry that is franchised, and in this case, something obviously went wrong at the office. One, the vehicle wasn't ready for pickup; two, equipment was missing; and three, someone else's furniture was still in the back. We were moving from our old house to our new house and our schedule was pretty tight that day.

Staff members were very apologetic, and our customer service guy sent someone out right away to pull out the furniture and get the things I ordered into the truck. Fifteen minutes later I was on my way.

But that was a foreshadowing of our ill-fated misadventure.

I drove the truck to our old house no problem and loaded it up. When I was ready to take everything over to the new house, I turned the key in the ignition and . . . *nothing*. The battery had died. Not only that, but the check engine light came on, so the truck clearly had a few issues. Luckily, I was able to use the app to let service know what was happening and I also called them on the phone to schedule roadside assistance. Unfortunately, I was stuck in the phone queue for more than an hour waiting for a customer service rep. Customers should *never* have to wait that long just to talk to a customer service rep, especially when their vehicle or product has broken down, but alas, as we all know, this is not all that unusual.

Fortunately, I was parked in front of my old house, and the truck was in a safe location. I didn't have to worry about someone running into it. But I could imagine if someone were driving their vehicle on a dark, busy, or rainy freeway and it broke down there. Waiting an hour or more to get put through to a customer service rep could quite literally turn what was just an inconvenience into tragedy.

When I finally got put through to a service rep, I explained the situation and was told that roadside assistance was on the way—they should arrive in about half an hour. The rep also explained that I could track their arrival using the app on my phone. Again, I thought, "Great! What a handy thing to have."

Score one for digital.

I checked the app every five minutes or so and received regular text alerts as the arrival time counted down. When the clock was down to about a minute to go, I was feeling relieved. I'd get my jump start and be back on the road soon.

The timer hit zero, and then it went negative. What?!? Minutes passed.

I thought, "This is even worse." I called the customer service number again, and this time it took me 35 minutes to get through to a rep. I had sent some texts too in response to the alerts. In my desperation, I was throwing everything I could think of at the wall, hoping something would stick. The rep then confirmed that something had gotten messed up with the roadside assistance, but that help would be on the way as soon as possible. They would send a new roadside assistance mechanic ASAP. I obviously wasn't a happy camper.

In the meantime, I decided I had had enough of waiting, so I looked for another way to remedy the situation. I remembered that the garage around the block where we normally park had a portable battery charger. I went there and asked the guy—we're friends—if I could borrow the machine to jump-start the truck. He offered to help, and he wheeled the battery charger over to our house. He gave the dead battery a quick charge and the truck started right up. By that time, I had lost at least two more hours of my time trying to get back on the road. I drove the truck to our new house, and I later found out that roadside assistance had finally arrived 10 minutes after I left.

I completed the move and needed to drop off the truck at the rental lot. It was after hours and dark by then—I was running several hours later than I planned—but they left the yard open for drop-offs. The lot was located on the western side of Chicago in an industrial area that is fairly desolate at night. The lot itself was below grade, making it a little intimidating at night, and no one was there but me. At least I hoped that was the case.

I had to use the app again to return the truck. The app instructed me to use a QR code plastered on the side of the building to initiate the return. Just one problem: the QR code didn't work because it was too dark—there was no lighting on the building. I even tried my phone flash but that didn't work either.

Take away that earlier point I gave to digital.

There I was, all by myself in the dark, and I couldn't for the life of me get the app to automatically initiate the drop-off process. I finally went into the app and found a work around to manually start the drop-off process. I had to take and upload photos of the inside and outside of the truck, where it was parked, the odometer and fuel gauge readings, and more. Not a one-and-done kind of thing by any means.

As I was working my way through the app, I was painfully aware of the fact that I wasn't situationally aware of what was going on around me. I was too busy concentrating on trying to get the app to work to notice if someone had wandered into the lot. The app wasn't functioning the way it needed to function and I was getting increasingly frustrated (the entire day had been an exercise in frustration). Every time I thought I was done with the drop-off process, the app would tell me to take a photo of something else or fill in some additional information. It just went on and on and on.

The Law of Unintended Consequences

This was a case where the moving truck rental company clearly intended to make people's lives easier through a better digital experience—customers can pick up and drop off their truck without all the usual paperwork or waiting in line, and the company doesn't need to have employees manning their lots 24/7.

But the reality was nowhere near the intention.

Instead of making customers' lives easier, the company was actually making their lives harder. The company's systems—both human and virtual—should have been more flexible meeting both real human needs and business goals.

The company's intent was good, but its execution was not. And it wasn't just customers' lives that were made harder, employees had to suffer too. After waiting on the side of the road for more than an hour to connect with a customer service rep,

I'm sure many customers let the reps know in no uncertain terms just how frustrated they were.

The People Quotient

From what I've seen, the more technology companies put into trying to make people's lives better, many of them are not thinking empathetically about what the repercussions are of either getting it wrong or not fully thinking it through. That's why I suggest the idea of building into these processes and customer touchpoints mini release valves that can expedite, clarify, and more.

Accomplishing this requires better technology and data, but it also requires a commitment to humanizing the organization—injecting the *people quotient* into the equation and redistributing the relative power of the C-suite with frontline managers and employees to improve the customer experience. I would go so far as to recasting the CEO as the *chief community officer* because the company is only as healthy as the community it represents—customers, employees, vendors, shareholders, and other stakeholders.

Let me go one step further: *Every* key executive from the top down needs to have their role recast to some degree to reflect the importance of the people quotient so they can honestly say, "I have personally gone through this myself, and here's what it feels like to be our customer—it's not great. Let's figure out a way to make it better."

But they need to be empowered to do so, and all need to recognize that technology and data can be used as tools for this purpose but are not a unilateral solution for it. Do this and I believe it would be far more powerful than doing more focus group surveys. It's the difference between telling a story as a movie or looking at a snapshot in time.

The organizational construct for this idea is very different from today's distinct operational groupings. It's the blur I talked about earlier in this chapter, which requires breaking down the walls between groups and thinking about every customer touchpoint as an opportunity to strengthen the brand, influence loyalty, and drive faster innovation. A fluid, agile team of people is needed who span across all those different touchpoints and operational elements. They see themselves as marketers, salespeople, technologists, data scientists, and service advocates.

This blur enables the organization to share insights and take action faster. Individuals have a travel passport for the organization and they can say, "Wait a minute. We're bombarding these people with marketing messages that say, 'we stand for this.' And in truth, there's no evidence that we do. We're not following through." Or they can say, "We sent people these offers, but they found them to be irrelevant and irritating, so they tuned them out. How are we going to fix that?" Or they might say, "We sold our customer a product, and if they have a problem with it after they bought it, they're mostly on their own—we're not stepping in to help. That doesn't make sense."

I know that it's complicated. You may have 15 different types of technology that all have to be knitted together, and you may have seven different groups that deal with these things because that's just the way the organization grew up. But honestly, it shouldn't be that way. We should be able to go to the chief executive officer and say, "We've got to change this today— right *now*." Maybe we've got to streamline it. Maybe it isn't always putting more people on it—instead, it might be that we need to provide customers with better access to the information they most typically search for.

Whatever it takes, it should be the full-time job of the chief community officer and their team to seek out points of customer dissatisfaction and frustration and get them fixed. Only then can you truly begin to humanize digital.

Get It Fixed

One time, when I was working with a large retail organization, I looked at their social accounts to see what customers were posting about their experiences with the company. Based on the posted comments, the feedback this organization was getting from customers was loud and clear: there was something wrong with the commerce experience.

I brought this to the attention of leadership and others in the organization. "I'm seeing lots of bad customer experiences on the social channels," I said. "Something's wrong."

The uniform response was, "We know about these things, and we've already fixed them."

Based on what I was continuing to see on the company's social, reviews, and feedback forums, this was not the case at all, so I decided to dig a little deeper.

I was working with a partner who was scaling machine learning and they wanted to do something with us to prove it out. I asked the partner if I could give them all the unstructured feedback we were getting just from the company's website—not social, but the website itself—and if they could come back with a ranking of the most common problems. They said, sure, they would run through all the data and give us the top-three issues out of a thousand.

They took the flat file of every comment that was on the website, and then they ran it through their machine-learning processing capability. And sure enough, when they came back with their report, of all the things I had been told were already fixed, not even one of them had been.

The top three customer complaints were things along the lines of, "I buy something and then you tell me, three weeks later, you don't have it in stock. What am I going to do now?" Or, "I put something in my cart and it disappeared." Or, "My promo code wasn't applied when I got to the cart." These seem like pretty straightforward stuff from a technical point of view, but very irritating to customers.

I feel that we genuinely believe we have solved these kinds of problems because we humans naturally think very linearly. "I was given a to-do, I did it, and therefore it's fixed." But we are not empowering people to go back and actually be the customer—to be on their side and ask, "Did we *really* fix it? Did we *really* make it better? Did we *really* do something that's in our customers' interests?" "Was the innovation that we innovated *really* that earth shattering, or did it just create an added layer of complexity?"

I honestly don't think you're going to get to that point unless you have someone who can play the role of chief whip. Not just from a customer perspective, but from an employee one as well—they both go together.

And I think they have to be able to swoop around and create a little chaos, not unlike the Chaos Monkey Netflix developed to randomly create failures in production systems to ensure no one gets too complacent in the status quo. Only then will stuff really get done and customers and employees get the attention—and the solutions—they deserve.

My UK Summer Adventure (I Think I'm Just Unlucky Renting Vehicles)

Before you think all my personal experiences with brands have been bad ones, I'm going to tell you a story about an experience where some empathy went a very long way for me personally. Yes, the overall experience was a bad one, and digital didn't help, but an empathetic person jumped in to make it much better when we needed her help the most.

When I was in college in the UK, my parents would come over every summer and we'd rent a car and drive around the island. They would usually set up the rental and take care of everything and I would serve as the driver. Because at the time I wasn't particularly savvy with how to drive a manual transmission car on the opposite side of the road (a lot to think about if you don't already have the required muscle memory), my parents' one request was that the car have an automatic transmission. Automatics weren't readily available for rent, however, and they had to be ordered long in advance.

One summer, my parents flew into Heathrow, and after we picked up their bags, I took them to the car rental office. I believe the company had just set up their UK operations and was having teething issues. We're reasonably patient people and we don't get easily flustered, but after waiting for an hour in a queue that wasn't moving an inch, it was clear something was not quite right.

I asked what was going on and found out that their computer systems were down. They had to send the agents out to the car park to grab each car and drive it to the office with the keys after they did the paperwork. We understood that things go wrong, so we weren't too upset about the situation. We eventually made it to the front of the queue and handed over our reservation paperwork for the automatic vehicle.

The rental agent's face suddenly drained, and he said, "Well, we don't actually have this car. We have a manual transmission car if you want to get that."

No, we didn't want to get that.

I told the agent, not entirely in jest, "If you want the car back with gears, you probably need to find us an automatic." Trying to be charming.

"Sorry," replied the agent, "but we don't have one."

"When do you think you'll have the car that we reserved— the one with an automatic transmission?" I asked.

"We'll have to wait for them to come in," the agent said, with an air of indifference. "Maybe in an hour, maybe in four, I have no idea."

By this point, the rental agency manager had walked up behind the agent. I asked the manager, and I was very calm about it, "Do you have *any* automatic transmission cars right now?"

"Yes," said the manager, "we do have one. But it's a luxury vehicle."

"Okay," I suggested, "why don't you give us that one?"

My usual experience with car rental companies in the United States is that if they have a car that meets your needs, and they have dropped the ball in some way, they will give you an immediate upgrade to get you on our way. Okay, I know that doesn't always fly everywhere; we can be a little spoiled in the United States. But while it's not a perfect situation for the company—they'll probably lose money on the deal—they're going to have a happy customer who's going to be on their way and maybe even post a nice review, come back the next time, and recommend the brand to friends through the stories they tell.

But the manager stuck to the letter of the law as she understood it. In the meantime, other people in the queue were getting into shouting matches with the agency staff about *their* vehicles. It was a really bad scene. I wouldn't stand down, though. I wasn't getting angry and I didn't lose it with them, but I wasn't going to just wait in the corner.

About two minutes later, another woman who worked for the rental agency came over to see if she could help. She had come over from the United States to help set up their new operation.

She whispered to me, "Here are the keys, here's your paperwork, now just go." We thanked her profusely. She fixed our problem, and we were on our way—in the car with an automatic transmission that the manager wouldn't let us have unless we paid a premium. Her action was empathy personified.

But we're not done with this story quite yet.

After driving all over the UK, and having a terrific time, we brought the car back 10 days later. The woman who had helped us was still there—she was doing all the paperwork. She recognized us and we thanked her again. "Thank you so much for helping us—you made my parents' trip really special. Do we owe you any extra for the upgrade?"

"No, no, no," the woman replied. "But if you could write a note to our head office, that would be really helpful."

"We're happy to do that, but why are you asking?" I wondered.

"When you left with the car 10 days ago," she said, "the manager tried to get me fired for giving you the keys."

"That's crazy," I told her. "You did something that was right. You felt empowered to do it. You probably *were* empowered because you came from the central office. But the manager tried to do you a dirty because you helped a customer."

And 19-year-old me did write a note—to the company's CEO. And, to my surprise, he wrote a really nice note back. He said, "I looked into this, and you should never have had this experience; none of our customers should. I know the employee in question and she's fantastic, that's why we sent her to the UK. We're thinking of promoting her." At the bottom of the letter was a coupon for a free rental for five more days.

My point is, we are all people with the same hopes, aspirations, and frustrations, but we don't always feel empowered to help get something done, to make it right. We're afraid to draw outside the lines to make the technologies, systems, and processes work the way they should—in the interests of our customers, employees, and management. It's a major missed opportunity and the result is a lot more angst and problems and costs.

Whatever your position may be—CEO, CMO, CIO, VP of sales, manager, and so on—empower people to do right by your customers. Be empathetic to their plight. Solve their problems then and there. But you must bake this reflex into the DNA of the organization, otherwise no one will feel enabled and there won't be a vehicle for employees to use to take action if they do.

And consider having your CEO take on the role of chief community officer—someone who continuously pulls back the covers on your organization, looking for problems like the one we experienced at Heathrow and ensuring they don't happen again.

Reducing Your Customers to Tears Is Not a Great Experience

My wife and I had our first baby when we were living in New York. Looking back, this was a very exciting time for us. Our lives were on the precipice of momentous change—we didn't know what to expect, we didn't know what we needed. Every day there were new questions for us to get answers to. We figured that getting registered at a store for the stuff we needed to take care of our new arrival would be one of the easiest things for us to do. The company's machine must be well-oiled, right?

We decided to get signed up on the Babies "R" Us gift registry, and we headed over to the Union Square anchor store in Manhattan. After we arrived and tried to get registered, we quickly realized that things weren't going well at all.

The registry computer systems weren't working—one woman was in a full-on meltdown because they might have deleted her account. They had devices you could carry around the store to scan items into your registry, and those things weren't working either. We were beginning to wonder if they were real. It was a bit like Chris O'Dowd in the comedy series *The IT Crowd* tricking his boss into thinking his computer was set up with voice commands. Chris's boss spent the rest of the episode screaming into his mouse.

In addition, none of the inventory tags were set up correctly. And to add insult to injury, we had to wait a long time just to get set up on the registry.

Here, Babies "R" Us had people streaming in who wanted to be their customers, and yet the company hadn't figured out how to make that experience as pleasant as they possibly could.

Having a baby is one of the most joyful things in life, and you don't want to burst anyone's bubble or give them a reason to never return. If you do the right things for the right people at the right time, you can derive a nice income stream from people who will be loyal to you forever because they had a great experience.

Sadly, on that day, in that Babies "R" Us, we were all having a *terrible* experience.

Afterward, I went home, and instead of writing an irate letter or calling customer service to complain, I jotted down some notes about our experience. For every issue enumerated, I also added in a potential solution. I managed to find the CEO's email address—he was an alumnus from my consulting days. I didn't know him personally, but I was able to track down his email address and send him a note.

I explained in my note that I wasn't trying to criticize the company (my general rule is fix the problem not the blame), I just wanted to give them some ideas for how to make the experience better. From better management of inventory and scanner systems, to appointment scheduling, to social media and reviews, I gave him my thoughts on how to be a bit more empathetic and why that might actually return real value.

I sent him an email that Saturday, and that evening he got back to me. "This is terrible," he said. "I talked with my direct reports about this, and it totally makes sense. I see this stuff too. What you're saying is sensible and I would like you to come visit me at headquarters to discuss further." Man, I didn't expect that kind of response, but looking back, a good CEO would take the time to follow up and should be deeply connected to their customers and employees.

You see these kinds of challenges day in and day out with any organization that you care to mention—even the best of them. And the bigger the organizations are, the more challenging the problems can be to resolve.

What You Can Do (Today)

My point still stands: if someone—or a group of someones—is appointed as a people-centric, empathetic weight in an organization, then the customer and employee experience will naturally improve. It's kind of the new version of what used to be market research. Instead of just thinking about the statistical aspects and abstracts of segments and customers, and doing a bunch of multivariate regressions to get to what motivates people in their demand, I believe the most basic thing is to walk in their shoes for a day and see what you learn. That's what the best shopkeepers were naturally able to do a century ago.

Go to the store, spend some time walking the aisles, visit the website, play with the chatbot, place an order online, run through the phone app, and do all the things your customers do. I'm sure there are people who do that in most organizations, but I don't know that they're empowered in terms of what they are able do when they run into problems. Can they go back and say, "All right, here is what I found, so before we do anything else we're changing this today!"? I don't think so. That has to be the *quid pro quo*.

Part of the problem is we don't always know where to start. Enterprise initiatives are more often than not episodic, partly because of the way they are organized, partly because of all the stuff that can get in the way. Technology that we hope will automate and make simple our most complex business problem fails to help us achieve our goals. And data that we covet because of insights it can deliver drowns us in the flood.

When you look at data in particular, it's kind of like that classic episode of *I Love Lucy* about Lucy and Ethel's first day of work at a chocolate factory. Their job was to take chocolates off a moving conveyor belt, package them in a paper wrapper, then put the finished candies back on the conveyor belt. Their supervisor explained that if a *single* chocolate got past them, they would be fired. Everything was going fine—at least until the conveyor belt started to go faster. In a futile attempt to keep up, Lucy and Ethel started eating the candy, stuffing it into their hats and clothing, and letting it drop onto the floor. They got away with it for a bit, but their supervisor was so impressed with the job they did that she ordered the conveyor belt to be sped up, making the problem even worse.

It's the same in today's business environment. All that data that everybody wants and says is so important becomes a flood that no one can keep up with. It falls on the floor and no one does anything with it because it has a sell-by date, just like those chocolates. So, if you're not feeding that information back into the organization and into your empathy team so that they can go and tap someone on the shoulder and say, "This stops today" or "This improves today," then I don't think you're taking this seriously.

How, then, do we get this done?

Someone needs to be the tiebreaker—someone who can reset and rebalance the power differential based on real-time insights, and who is always in the customer's and in the employee's corner. That someone is ideally your CEO/chief community officer, assisted by technology for sure. Otherwise, you'll keep repeating the same things, time after time after time, and wondering why you aren't getting different outcomes. As the old saying goes (often misattributed to Einstein), "Insanity is doing the same thing over and over again and expecting different results."

So, why are we waiting? Why aren't we setting ourselves up to be best in class to get there first, to be doing the right things for the customer, for the employee, from day one?

Good question! If you do, then you will build a better company—a company that will be more profitable over the long term because you'll attract the right people to be your customers and the best people to work for you. That's just not happening in many organizations today. I understand that we're moving really fast and everything's at scale, and making the wrong tweak could cost you millions. But that's very short-term thinking. If you treat people badly—or even worse, neglect them—you'll make them feel like they don't matter and you're going to reap what you sow. They will walk.

And remember: research shows that it's somewhere between 5 and 25 times more expensive to gain a new customer than it is to retain one you've already got.[2] *Employee Benefit News* (*EBN*) reports that it costs employers 33 percent of a worker's annual salary to hire a replacement if that worker leaves, excluding productivity losses.[3]

You could burn through tons of dollars to try to attract someone new, or you could spend a little bit of money and give the customer and employee a kiss on the cheek in a proactive way and just hold onto them. As Walt Disney once said, "Whatever you do, do it well. Do it so well that when people see you do it, they will want to come back and see you do it again, and they will want to bring others and show them how well you do what you do."[4]

Shouldn't *your* organization be known for doing the same?

4

The Battle for Trust in the Digital Age—The More We See, the Less We Believe

Trust is the glue of life.
It's the most essential ingredient in effective communication.
It's the foundational principle that holds all relationships.

—Stephen Covey

In the 1950s and 1960s, we were very much in the *Mad Men* era of marketing, which was all about being clever and resonating with people who you intuited or divined were your audience. There were lots of broad statements made about large segments of the population, such as the familiar "What's good for General Motors is good for America" or this 1964 ad for Samsonite Silhouette luggage: "Silhouette is you ... slender, fast-paced, daringly elegant."[1]

These statements and slogans were the fundamental elements of trust. Customers received the brand promise—it was usually simple, and the reality of the experience might have been hit or miss. Reviews, forums, social, and modern channels didn't exist for consumers, so you relied on authoritative figures or pitchmen to provide the confidence.

In truth, the American population was not as homogeneous as marketers thought it was, and people weren't quite as receptive to the kinds of broad statements that many marketers were routinely making. As it turned out, the American Dream *could* be segmented into a lot of different pieces. In addition, the concepts of need states and behaviors versus expectations also came into play, further parsing customer segments.

As the digital age started to take hold, the premise of a universally held brand promise that everyone trusted became increasingly hard to maintain. Given all the outlets for customers, employees, and other influencers to share and compare experience, a brand today is what your community of interest says it is and it's only as good as the preponderance of evidence may suggest.

Initially, marketers and business leaders thought about only one side of the equation (in the traditional terms, the one they knew—broadcast marketing), "Ooh, marvelous! For the first time we can get all this data on people, and with it we can pinpoint our marketing messages to them more directly."

With the advent of email (many observers mark the birth of digital marketing to the day in 1971 when Ray Tomlinson sent the very first email message), and as we add more channels to the mix, what made digital marketing different from traditional marketing was primarily the delivery method. Unfortunately, for all the promise, what stayed the same was the old-school thinking firmly rooted in the early-twentieth-century mindset. That never really shifted.

Marketers thought, "If we only had *this* data, we would be able to do everything and be mega successful." In truth, it's a lot harder than that. It's not so much about how many pieces of customer data you can accumulate—gigabytes, terabytes, petabytes, and so on. It's about the *context*, it's about where someone is in their decision-making and in their journey, it's about who gives them the confidence to buy something or to engage with a brand. As powerful as the insights we gain from analyzing marketing data can be, there are still a lot of things going on in the human mind that can't always be accounted for just by getting a better database.

Even now, you can see that with every new channel, with every new social, modern channel account platform, the stakes and the lexicon that marketers use is still the same: How do we define success through reach or how do we define success through engagement? But what's lost in that is the idea that if only we knew a little bit more about the customer, we'd be able to reach them with the right marketing message, with the right offer, with the right product or service.

And in truth, it has turned out to be frightfully more complex than that. But this sort of vision for the future still exists—just as it did in the post-World War II period—that Americans' lives would be so much better. We would work less, be happier, and all these remarkable new technologies would make our lives simpler and better. Well, this vision didn't exactly pan out the way it was supposed to. The truth to the contrary, these new technologies, one could argue have made our lives more complex, more disrupted, and less fulfilled while undermining trust.

When you look back across fairly recent history, the introduction of major new technologies has often been accompanied by much trepidation and warnings based on the anticipated disruption they were predicted to cause to the social fabric. There is a natural fear and skepticism. Indeed, with each new technology came potential resistance for fear of what it might do to society, to industries and social structures.

Soon after telephones started to become widely available, there were concerns that this new technology would increase the speed at which people would have to react in their day-to-day interactions. According to an article in an 1899 British newspaper, "The use of the telephone gives little room for reflection. It does not improve the temper, and it engenders a feverishness in the ordinary concerns of life which does not make for domestic happiness and comfort."[2] In other words, telephones might steal away a bit of our humanity—perhaps turning us into unfeeling machines or automatons.

Of course, more recent major technologies have also been accused of being disruptive to the social fabric (which has already been disrupted numerous times by previous tech innovations). While texting in particular has attracted much concern—from distracted drivers to distracted mates to distracted students—the same has also been true for the arrival of email, the internet, and the social web. In each case, people become more closely wedded and attentive to their electronic devices than to the people sitting right next to them. Again, one could argue, a bit of our humanity is stolen by the next technical gadget or medium—at least that's the concern voiced by many observers.

You could certainly make the argument that every consumer technology has isolated us a bit more, despite all the many benefits each has brought to us. The vision for product developers and manufacturers has been to make our lives better and easier, and for marketers, to make their messages more targeted and more impactful. But in reality, all the technologies we're using are changing to a certain degree the way we relate and interact and think—how we prioritize certain things that we used to take for granted. Our technologies are changing us and how we see and interact with the world and with those around us.

And then consider the impact of major disruptions *not* of our invention, such as the COVID-19 virus. Employees who used to be in close quarters with one another were suddenly torn out of their offices and workplaces and moved into their homes—often with spouses and children who had been torn out of *their* jobs and schools. This change in social dynamics, which occurred almost literally overnight, was facilitated by digital communications platforms such as Slack, Microsoft Teams, and Zoom. And it's fundamentally changed how business leaders think about the future of work.

I'm sure a lot of business leaders are thinking right now, "Hey, we kinda got away with not having everybody in the office—maybe we can keep this good thing going." Of course, there are others who think the reverse, "We've got to get people back in the office as quickly as possible—they're not getting as much done working at home!" And workers are often caught in the middle. Many now expect to be able to continue their remote work status, and if they can't, they assume it's because their employers don't trust them.

All this could be chalked up to the change that circumstances force us to confront, but it also requires us to stop and think about the long game. Do we go with the flow because we are riding the next big wave, or do we have an obligation to question and make a concerted stance on what we believe is good for customers, employees, and society, and how we will therefore act? This is the new brand promise, and how we frame it will directly affect how trusted we are as an organization.

We're at a surprising split in many ways between what we thought the digital vision of the future would be and where we actually are today. We thought all this data would make our lives so much easier as marketers, as business leaders, as communicators, but in truth it's just made things more complex and uncertain. Now we need to think more carefully about what *kind* of data is important and to separate the wheat from the chaff and get rid of the unimportant data because it gets in the way.

We also, more than ever, need to agree how we use data, how we manage it, what promises we make to customers and employees, and how we follow through on those promises. Technology and data are two-way streets; the more data collected, the more opportunity for misinformation, the more uncertainty around what a brand stands for, the more opportunity for mistrust.

People are clearly anxious about how data about them is used. Accenture's Tech Vision research revealed that two-thirds of consumers (66 percent) say they're as concerned about the commercial use of their personal data and online identity for personalization purposes as they are about security threats and hackers.[3] According to a McAfee survey, 43 percent of people feel they lack control over their personal data, and 33 percent aren't certain they can control how businesses collect it.[4] People are also concerned about companies that link their data to advertising. Seventy-seven percent of respondents in a 2019 survey reported that they were uncomfortable when they noticed targeted online ads.[5] Not only that, but according to an RSA Security global survey, only 17 percent of people consider personalized ads to be ethical.[6]

Results like these are a tremendous problem for companies, and it shows just how much trust consumers feel when they are on the receiving end of personalized online ads. When people don't trust a company, they will seek out companies they do trust. In fact, an Accenture survey found that 58 percent of consumers reported they would switch 50 percent or more of their spending to companies that provided excellent, personalized experiences that did not compromise their trust.[7]

Many businesses are taking positive steps to shore up the trust consumers feel toward them. In just one example, quick-serve giant McDonald's is providing employees greater control over their workplace, allowing them to change menu displays based on local conditions, utilizing live traffic data, observation of peak customer demand, and more.[8] This change at McDonald's promises to make the experience better for both customers and employees.

We have to think about the different types of data we gather as the key for understanding the needs of a customer. No matter what you do or how clever you get with the data—you can conduct all the multivariate analyses and regressions you like—at the end of the day, if you ignore the basic principles of what makes us human, you do so at your own peril. And you miss a tremendous opportunity to humanize digital.

The Great (Digital) Divide

The *digital divide* is often talked about in socioeconomic terms—the people who can afford the hardware required to access the internet, and those who cannot. That's not the kind of digital divide I'm talking about here. At the 50,000-foot level, there's the digital divide that separates us as humans from the machine world. The machine world keeps growing and we keep trying to perfect it, and we erroneously think that it's predicated on understanding every aspect of human behavior through data.

But there's still the human, nondescript, poetical side of the divide, which is hard to quantify in purely mathematical terms. This side of the divide owes more of its origins and its power to the fact that human behavior is incredibly complex and constantly changing. However, there are things that don't change because they're specific to our species. There are things that we have accreted over time that prevent us from being a perfect fit for whatever marketing models someone comes up with. As a result, despite all we do to organize ourselves and organize society and organize our customers, we're in truth not very organized at all. Trying to organize that chaotic bit on the other side of organization is what creates a stark demarcation line between the digital world and the human world.

The divide creates an omnipresent tension that I don't think people pay a lot of attention to. The tension is there when we see something that's an outlier, such as a massive data breach that outrages millions of customers, or we visit a website and it feels kind of creepy because we're getting asked a lot of personal questions, or we engage in a debate about how much of our so-called personal information is actually personal. See the visualization below on the five rising areas of consumer motivation when making purchase decisions.[9] These five rising areas are quickly displacing quality and price, and they're at that demarcation line between what's digital and what's human. As such, if not addressed adequately by brands, they have the potential to undermine faith in the business and its products or services.

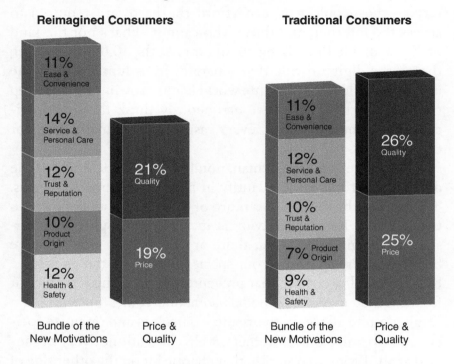

Reimagined Consumers

- 11% Ease & Convenience
- 14% Service & Personal Care
- 12% Trust & Reputation
- 10% Product Origin
- 12% Health & Safety

- 21% Quality
- 19% Price

Bundle of the New Motivations   Price & Quality

Traditional Consumers

- 11% Ease & Convenience
- 12% Service & Personal Care
- 10% Trust & Reputation
- 7% Product Origin
- 9% Health & Safety

- 26% Quality
- 25% Price

Bundle of the New Motivations   Price & Quality

But what if you pivot away for a moment from the struggle between digital and human, and instead think about the two being blended together as one and the same? Once we accept that the first order of importance for any organization is to support the human, not the data, then how do we make the digital experiences we have conform to something that's a little bit more fluid and a little bit more abstract and a little bit more humanized—something that really works in terms of engaging customers and citizens?

At every point in human history, there's been distrust of the machine. One group might call each successive technology progress while another group might call it disenfranchisement. And it never stops. From the telephone to email and texting to social media to the internet of things to artificial intelligence—that tension has always been there and there's always going to be that debate. The challenge for bringing detente is being able to make sure that one aids the other, rather than the other way around.

I believe that right now we are at an inflection point. There are some very weighty issues plaguing us because of our digital progress as humans, and it's not certain which paths we will take and if they will turn out to be the right ones.

How far does digital lead us away from our natural instincts as humans, and does it support us or does it threaten us? You would think that by having digital experiences that help people discover things, help people learn, help people connect—you can go down the list of 30 different things that digital can do—that weight of digital would clearly be overwhelmingly on the side of good. But there's a polar element to it that we struggle with, which is that, for as much information as digital brings to us, it now also raises the specter of whether we can trust that information. How do we know that what we're discovering is actually true?

We used to enjoy and be entertained by marketing messages, but now we're starting to get the feeling that they're insidious, invasive, perhaps even a little bit evil. For the most part, we increasingly ignore them, so all the effort and investment is falling on deaf ears. But when we do pay attention, we think marketers might just know something about us that we don't know about ourselves, and that can be really scary. When they follow us all around the internet, when we buy something—or *think* about buying something—and all of a sudden we're getting targeted marketing messages. When they keep trying to sell us what we already bought, it can feel like Big Brother is watching us very closely. In fact, a 2020 survey of consumers in the United States, the UK, Australia, Spain, France, and Japan reported that two-thirds of respondents felt that ads that followed them across devices were "creepy."[10]

Then there's the whole issue of who controls technology and for what purpose. We like to think that the internet was constructed as a happy-go-lucky, open-source fount of all wisdom for everyone. And originally it was—that was the charter. There were a bunch of well-meaning scientists and engineers who created a vision for the internet, and their goal was to make it noncommercial and open for everyone to use. It was very Summer of Love. Everyone felt empowered because they didn't know much about it, and *no one* knew much about it, and so the playing field was somewhat equal.

But as every technology proceeds, that equality naturally erodes and we arrive at a place where some people and organizations are more equal than others, while the vast majority are less equal. I don't control the internet. I don't control my internet service provider (ISP). I don't know what an ISP is. I don't know who has data on me. I don't know how they got that data on me. And I don't know how to manage that. I don't even know what it's worth. The fact of the matter is people are feeling less and less in control.

The same thing is true when it comes to social media. When social media took off, I was one of the first people to get excited about its promise. I was certain it would promote transparency and civil behavior. I think a lot of people believed that at the time. But as time has passed, we've seen over the past 10 years that more people are aware of what you can do with it—for both good and bad—and how you can manipulate and use it for your own benefit. There's a narrow band of people and institutions that can do that, while the vast majority of us cannot.

According to the Oxford Internet Institute's 2020 media manipulation survey, organized social media manipulation campaigns were found in all 81 of the countries surveyed—an increase of 15 percent over the previous year. In addition, the survey found that more than 93 percent of countries surveyed deploy disinformation as part of political communication. Says Oxford Internet Institute director Philip Howard:

Our report shows misinformation has become more professionalized and is now produced on an industrial scale. Now, more than ever, the public needs to be able to rely on trustworthy information about government policy and activity. Social media companies need to raise their game by increasing their efforts to flag misinformation and close fake accounts without the need for government intervention, so the public has access to high-quality information.[11]

You can see now where institutions and people who might have an alternative agenda have started to figure out how to play the angles. The result of that is increasing suspicion and distrust, uncertainty about who or what to believe (what is fact and what is propaganda), and a nagging suspicion that in the overall scheme of things, we can trust no one. We are confronted with the devastating realization that we don't matter all that much as individuals.

It's clearly in our interest as marketers, business leaders, and government leaders to close this digital divide, and to build trust with our citizens, customers, employees, partners, investors, and the communities in which we do business. I would argue that it is *essential* if we are to continue to advance as a society—*together*, not divided. As *partners*, not tribal adversaries.

The Threat to Markets and Capitalism

When technology is used for good—understanding that the definition of *good* is relative and subject to debate—it's readily apparent that it opens up doors and creates all kinds of new opportunities for people in all walks of life, young and old, in communities and countries all around the world. That's as true today as it has been for the past many thousands of years of human history. When early humans discovered how to make and contain fire, that led to much good—from cooking to creating warming fires to tool-making and much more. It helped us elevate ourselves from mere primates to rulers of the earth. Of course, in the hands of an arsonist (or the errant hooves of Mrs. O'Leary's cow), fire can also be a bad thing—destroying everything in its path.

The same is true for new technologies such as social media. Facebook has enabled billions of people around the world to forge digital connections with one another—to, in words of the company's mission statement, "give people the power to build community and bring the world closer together."[12] But the social media giant also, beginning in 2014, enabled Cambridge Analytica to harvest the personal data of more than 50 million Facebook users without their consent. The data was eventually used to great advantage by the successful presidential campaign of Donald Trump—microtargeting 10,000 different ads to a variety of Facebook audiences, which were viewed billions of times.[13]

Technology helps us grow as a society—it creates demand that was never there. It also makes the world a better place by banishing darkness; providing reliable transportation and communication; and improving our health, prosperity, and understanding of the world (and universe) around us. There are whole new markets, whole new businesses, whole new ways of working, whole new ways of thinking and creating that didn't exist 10 years ago, 5 years ago, last year.

That's the good part.

The bad part, which could threaten all of that, we as marketers, data scientists, engineers, technologists, and innovators need to understand is that the benefits don't always apply to all groups evenly, and the power that technology can engender doesn't flow equitably. If we don't take a step back and set aside some time to think about what it is that we're doing in a structured way, we may create so much distrust that we are unable to manage it. It's come full circle to the point where governments don't understand this well enough, or they understand only pieces of technology and digital, and they try to prescribe answers that may only solve part of the problem or make matters worse.

In my view, the essence of capitalism is to constantly reinvent, constantly creatively destroy, and constantly bring new ways of doing things to the fore. If you use this technology to protect versus to reinvent, then to me that is what ultimately undermines the growth and innovation that we've seen. Maybe the companies that were thought of as the scrappy start-ups have become behemoths. They suddenly realize that they're no longer as innovative as they once were, and they struggled to get back to their roots. You see it at its worst when organizations are anticompetitive, and that's a pervasive danger.

There has been a lot of talk lately about breaking up "Big Tech" companies such as Amazon, Google, and Facebook, asserting that they are monopolies. However, perhaps we shouldn't be too hasty when it comes to trying to tear them apart. While some may see political gain from demonizing these large companies, they aren't necessarily breaking any laws. Says Boston University Questrom School of Business professor, Michael Salinger, "You're only guilty of monopolization if you've attained your monopoly by means other than providing a better product at a better price. Look at Google. People want to search on Google. Their search yields useful information and it's free, so it's no wonder they've got such a strong position in the market."[14]

Says Boston University Questrom School of Business assistant professor, Garrett Johnson, "It's frustrating that the conversation tends to go along the lines of, 'These companies are doing bad things, so we want to hurt them by breaking them up.' If we start breaking up companies wantonly, that's going to hurt innovation."[15]

Is that the best way to improve trust?

There's no single way to solve this particular equation. I think it's going to require new ideas and new thoughts, but first a recognition that there's a potential problem. Even if it hasn't yet occurred in your organization, there's a potential problem.

And maybe we need to constantly have some sort of mechanism in place here, whether it's internal to an organization, or unique to an individual entrepreneur, or part of a state-sponsored way of thinking about reinventing what's right and wrong in terms of regulation. Those things need to be addressed and we must be very open about them.

I am often asked, "How can I use technology to be more innovative?" I think that's the wrong question. I think innovation has nothing to do with the technology or the technology platforms you may deploy, and it has everything to do with what kind of community you want to be and how you engage and motivate it. How are you going to attract and retain people who are really creative, and encourage them without stifling them? You don't want to disturb those mechanisms because that could damage your current operation or your current business.

Addressing Institutional Amnesia

If you chart the maturity path of any organization, there's probably a graph that looks very similar, no matter which institution it is. That's because it's a *human* journey. From someone with an idea to do something different, to address a longstanding problem, to right a wrong—whatever it may be. That person convinces a couple of other people to join them, thereby creating a start-up of some sort. It could be a new nonprofit organization or a new for-profit business that has the potential to grow and to have an impact on the world.

To scale, there are certain paths you need to take—certain controls you need to put into place and certain kinds of people you need to hire. And that maturity path probably looks very similar for every single company, institution, or even government that has ever existed. You can, for example, think of the United States as an interesting start-up with a bunch of somewhat cantankerous founders who had a revolutionary idea. They got together and kicked around their idea over tea and ale, building on it and gaining momentum.

I think what happens when organizations grow—when they go from start-up to being mature, multifaceted, and highly successful—they need to be more efficient and they need to watch their productivity. All good things in and of themselves, but where is the trust factor in this journey? It's often lost in the din of other priorities. I am not asking, "How do you ensure your leaders and employees are trustworthy?" I am asking, "How do you build and maintain the intimate trust of your core constituents, and how do you maintain it in spite of scale?" You do this through improved experiences and the flourishing of empathy at all levels.

As Accenture's report "Shaping the Sustainable Organization" explained, "Sustainable organizations are purpose-led businesses which inspire their people and partners to deliver lasting financial performance, equitable impact, and societal value that earns and retains the trust of all stakeholders."[16] To be sustainable and successful, you have to embed these behaviors and practices into the entire culture. Listen to stakeholders, be empathetic to their experiences, and truly take on their concerns and needs.

But what often gets forgotten is the thing that sparked the organization in the first place. And the spark comes from *people*. It comes from human ingenuity and creativity. It comes from visceral experiences we have that get us thinking. As organizations travel along the maturity path, at the apex of that curve, they suffer a form of institutional amnesia. They do so at their own peril because, chances are, they'll miss the writing on the wall. They'll miss the greatest opportunities to grow and innovate. They'll shy away from experiencing creative destruction and being reborn.

The organizations that get it right aren't afraid to take that risk. They make the leap when they arrive at the top of the apex of the maturity curve. It might look like they're destroying value, but in truth, they're getting closer to their human roots, the visceral needs that are in all of us. And as a result, they get closer to their customers again because they've had to think about how they do business completely from scratch.

What matters most to you in those moments are the human experiences. Even if you self-help, you find that in the process of doing it, the organization made it very easy for you—intuitive, smooth, and easy. It was empathetic and designed a process that met the needs of the human based on what issues, problems, and stumbling blocks they may be likely to encounter. It's not a question of, "I'm going to get rid of my call center and humans," it's "I'm just going to make that interaction a lot more valuable for all parties."

But there's a higher plane of trust: companies that put in place the right culture and behaviors to listen to customers and come up with the right products and services. And increasingly, they have to be bold. They need to think of creating a platform to grow their business. No point selling a furnace, you've got to sell household environmental experiences. No point selling cars, you've got to sell mobility and unique personalized destinations. It takes companies doing something profound—not just improving customer service and love, but having the determination and the courage to reinvent themselves. They recognize that they've got to share value with others in the ecosystem and blur the lines of operations, both within and without the organization.

I don't think of service as a separate function or endpoint, but a lot of organizations with few exceptions still do. They'll have a customer service group, and in my experience, customer service groups have got to be one of the most challenging experiences you could ever have. If you can survive being a customer care representative, you can probably survive anything. All day long, customer care reps are required to deal with people who are having serious issues—and those people are often frustrated, overworked, underappreciated, and even a bit angry about their plight.

That's not all that unusual—they're human. They are each of us and all of us. But in my view, this is one of the most valuable functions an organization can have. Indeed, my alma mater, Bloomberg, made it a core selling point—call their help center and they promise to pick up within two rings and connect you with a real person. They promise to solve your problem first time.

In the twenty-first century, those companies that really succeed will go back to the future. They'll realize that they need to be closer to their customers—not just because they think they know more about them, but because they are truly connected to them. They are part of a community that needs to act and engage like a community.

I think the ideal company of the future is not going to be rigidly segmented into different operational departments such as marketing, sales, service, manufacturing, or development. It's going to be everyone in the company as a marketer, salesperson, customer service agent, everyone having a hand in innovation, and so on. These are the best parts of how start-ups operate— everyone pitches in and learns about the customer and helps build a community of trust.

They should regularly walk a mile in a customer's shoes and really get to know them. Hiding away in some part of the organization and quietly doing their bit is going to be a luxury that no company can afford. They should all be able to tell you what three things they know about their most valuable customer that their competitor doesn't.

If that's the thesis, and if we think that's the way organizations are going to be successful, then everything is going to have to change in the way that information flows, how it's shared, and the intelligence and so-whats that are divined from it. When you do, if your customer has a problem, you can act or change direction faster—before it becomes a larger issue or missed opportunity. Not only in terms of pounds and pence, but it costs you in terms of brand trust. It's always less expensive to hold onto a customer than to get a new one, the same as it is with good employees. And the companies that suffer the most are the ones that do the math and realize that they're churning both. It's a zero-sum game. It erodes value over time.

I have a friend who worked for the chief marketing officer at SAP, which was traditionally a very structured organization. This fellow worked in social media, and it was the first role SAP had ever hired for someone to focus on social media. Social media was very worrisome to the majority of people who worked there because, at the time, there were only maybe two or three people in the entire organization who could speak outside the four walls of SAP about anything—who could talk to the customer extemporaneously. That clearly had to change.

A few years ago, SAP's CMO made a conscious decision that *everyone* was going to talk to customers and to be as open and transparent as they could possibly be. They realized that it was their job to help their customers—even if it was an esoteric or arcane request on a weird channel that typically wasn't the right channel to go through. That's how we are; humans are leaky buckets and the water is going to find its lowest level and go to wherever it needs to go. So why not recognize that and figure out how to build that intimacy across the entire organization so that everyone in the organization understands the customer?

The Digital Law of Diminishing Returns

I personally believe that the more obsessed you are with becoming "tech- and data-centric, agile, and innovative," the less successful you will actually be. It's about being *smart*, not checking the latest boxes someone says you need to check. It's about recognizing that there are a lot of things that you don't know about your most valuable customer that your competitors probably do. Again, there's that question that I never stop asking executives and myself: "What three things can you tell me about your most valuable customer that your competitors don't know?"

What about you? Can you name three things about your most valuable customer that your competitors don't know?

I'll guarantee that it's going to be a hard question for you to answer because we get so into the process, and we get so consumed with acquiring and churning through data, and we get so consumed with developing reports, that we often miss the forest for the trees.

I once traveled to one of Accenture's development centers in India to take a look at what the teams are doing there. It was fascinating—I was amazed at the work that is being done, for every brand you can mention. I talked with someone who was leading a social media team for a particular client, analyzing the performance of campaigns. "That's fascinating," I said to the team leader, "what exactly are you looking at?"

"We are measuring the impact of digital campaigns," the team leader said, "for example, the launch or content programs. The client wants to see that their money was well spent. They want to see their CPMs, how far their campaigns traveled, and how people engaged with or shared content."

"That's great," I continued. "What are the insights that came out of that? Did they learn about some new product that customers might be interested in, or a feature that they're looking for? Or did they learn that there was a problem that a sizable percentage of customers are dealing with? Or did you drive them to do something, like download a special coupon or sign up for an app or join a community—something tangible?"

"Well, no," replied the team leader. "The client isn't asking for us to do any of that."

"What are they asking for?" I wondered out loud.

"They just want an Excel spreadsheet with media reach and frequency," explained the team leader.

"There's a big, missed opportunity here," I said. "What if you could take a step back and just pause for a second and ask your client, 'What three things would you like to know about your most valuable customers or prospects that your competitors don't know? What would that be worth to you, particularly if you could execute against it?'"

Asking this question will help you pick out the most important and actionable targets and avoid getting drowned in a sea of data. Instead of experiencing decreasing returns on digital, your organization's effectiveness will increase exponentially.

Are Institutions Unprepared?

Despite the general belief that the majority of organizations are unprepared to build truly empathetic digital systems, saying that they're *all* unprepared is clearly not the case. Organizations are prepared in pockets, and the unpreparedness that's out there is mostly for taking the next leap—joining the dots together to build understanding and empathy for customers into the fabric and DNA of organizations.

When I was running social media for organizations, people would ask me, "What's the value of social?" My response was usually something along the lines of, "I think of social as being the solvent for an organization. It loosens up the bonds that you normally have and breaks down or melts the barriers between different parts of the organization—shining a light through the holes that it punches and giving you insights about the customer in real time."

When social opens up those holes, there should be a customer at the other end—a customer that you maybe never noticed, or engaged with, or learned something about. In fact, that customer might be just a mirror—it might be *you*.

Everyone who is a customer or a consumer is going to form an opinion about that organization based on the last conversation or interaction they've had with that brand. It's not what the brand tells you it is. It's not an abstract brand promise. It's not whether you were able to fulfill your orders on time or fulfill the price guarantee.

It's about what little thing did customers experience today in the interactions they had—whether online, offline, face-to-face, remote, in an email or chat—that will color their perspectives and perceptions of that brand, and in their own minds decide whether to engage with that brand again? That's the world we live in—that's what the digital solvent has done. You can hire as many agencies as you want to come up with fantastic and creative campaigns, and they can come up with wonderfully humorous or thought-provoking ads. But at the end of the day, it's not about the creative; rather, it's about whether you make a real connection with someone? Did you learn something about them? Did you drive a behavior that otherwise would not have been realized had you not made the effort?

Victoria Morrissey is chief marketing officer at Ferguson Enterprises, and before that served as global marketing and brand leader for Caterpillar. In an interview, she told me about the power of making connections with customers on their terms:

> *If you use Ferguson as an example, you get a lot more traction if you aren't the one imparting the knowledge, but you're the one enabling the connections.*
>
> *In my experience, the power of social media lies in uncovering and sharing the amazing customer and associate stories and using those stories and experiences to create a community linking others who are dealing with some of the same things. It was the idea of "it was brought to you by Ferguson or Caterpillar." It wasn't about the company imparting the knowledge, it was about unleashing the power that comes from connecting customers with others who were in the same boat they were.*
>
> *They want to learn from each other because those lessons are really, really valuable. And if you connect them, you get credit for building that relationship. The rest is history.*

The problem, I imagine, is that in many organizations, leaders are wedded to the past, to the status quo. They don't really know any better. One of the easiest things to embrace is inertia. Think about how hard it for us personally to try a new series on Netflix, though their algorithms do their best to present us with options the company thinks we'll like. It usually takes a lot of people nudging us before we'll try something new. It's much easier to just stick with what we already do and know.

If you're an executive, a CMO, or some other organizational leader, that's not good enough. You've got to be willing to take a risk if you hope to move the organization forward and to scale. The question that often gets in the way is this: Are you going to be willing to bet your career on doing something new? Something a bit daring? Are you willing to become a company that listens to customers and their human needs and creates products and services they really need—as well as deliver them in smarter ways?

Few executives get fired for doing the same thing over and over that has worked in the past. Even if that thing has less and less impact on growing and changing, evolving and innovating, and connecting with your existing and prospective customers. You're not going to get fired. You will (like the organization you work for) more likely fade away. For 100 years, Sears was *the* top retailer in the country—until they weren't. Amazon and other nimbler competitors ate their lunch.

As I have said often, Sears *should* have been Amazon—it *was* the Amazon of its time. There was not a corner on this continent communally glued together by a bigger brand than Sears. They taught us how to shop, and we evolved along with the brand—the company was an integral part of our social fabric and traditions. To then miss the boat on the next big thing—*why*? This was their DNA, this was who they were, this was how they were built.

You can go through every industry and examine each one and how the top brands are trying to scramble toward a digital world. But here's a cautionary note: in that scramble, don't just do stuff because you think it's important to do, and that you think you're going to be left behind because you didn't embrace technology soon enough or completely enough.

Whatever you do, whatever you've invested, don't lose sight of the most important thing, which is understanding the customer: new ones, old ones, existing ones, potential ones, former ones. That's what is going to drive everything that you do today and in the future—from process, to platform, to channel strategy, to marketing strategy, and on and on. You need to have a thirst for understanding the problems, trials, and travails of your consumers and customers—B2B or B2C—and then be able to empathetically design for people in the context of the ever-changing needs they have. Hold on to them by being a better and more understanding friend than anyone else.

That is how you build and retain trust.

That is how you continue to grow.

5

The Importance of Moving
from Predicting to Anticipating

*The present defines the future. The future builds on the foundation
of the past.*

—Lailah Gifty Akita

Ultimately, marketing is about telling stories. Some observers peg the beginning of marketing to the mid-1400s and Gutenberg's invention of the movable type printing press, which made mass printing of fliers, posters, and books far faster, easier, and less expensive than existing printing methods. However, I believe the origins of marketing can be traced back even further, to the prehistoric humans who first started using tools.

At some point after they gained the ability to speak with one another, these early humans started to make small cave paintings of wild animals, other humans, and even stencils of their own hands. They used these paintings and other forms of art to tell stories that would connect them more closely with their family and members of their tribe or clan, and to leave something behind.

So, if you think about this as core to marketing, which is to tell stories about the aspirations, the momentous occasions, and the needs that people may have—whether you're selling toothpaste or a car or a home—I believe marketing today has its roots in our prehistoric past.

Just after Hurricane Sandy devastated New York and New Jersey, I was asked to make a presentation on social media. I was in a new role at Bloomberg, and until I was hired, the company had forbidden social media. I needed to come up with a theme for the presentation, and I settled on "Don't be afraid of social media." My goal was to make social media less frightening to the folks at Bloomberg.

The heart of my message was, "Yes, social media is typically an extemporaneous, stream-of-consciousness kind of conversation and everyone can see it. But in truth, the guardrails are baked into our human DNA in the sense that we're still trying to do the same thing we always have, which is to connect with people, tell stories, and build community."

I'll never forget a photograph published in *Time* magazine, taken in the aftermath of Sandy. The photo was of the inside of a Chase Bank in Midtown Manhattan, with a crowd of people sheltering next to the ATM machines—my guess is that it was one of the few places in the city with backup power. Everyone was sitting on the floor in a circle, with their smartphones and laptops plugged into the bank's AC outlets.[1] They built an instant community.

The scene reminded me of the standard illustration we've all seen in our history books of Neolithic humanoids, sitting around a fire and sheltering from the elements and wild animals. Even though we don't have written records from those long-ago times, it's easy to imagine that as they sat around the fire, they were telling stories and building camaraderie and community. They were entertaining one another, keeping people in line, and passing on their culture. They were showing their family and friends that they mattered.

Fast forward to the post-COVID world of today. There's widespread fear that modern communication channels such as social media are breaking us apart because they allow us to have our own echo chamber. But I believe, at its most elemental, when you strip away all the digital aspects of these experiences, you still get to what's most important to people: to know that they matter and to know that they're leaving something behind for future generations. In previous centuries, we used to put it in a diary. Today, we post what's most important in our daily lives to our Instagram or Facebook or TikTok.

I think it's time for us as marketers, executives, and communicators to go back to the future.

When I think about the idea of "back to the future," I think back to my father and his visits to the Marshall Field's department store in downtown Chicago where the toy department salesperson knew his name and couldn't wait to show him the latest products. Although we never talked about it, I'm certain my father felt really good that this salesperson built a connection with him and treated him as though he mattered. The salesperson didn't know *everything* about my father, but he knew enough to give my father the impression that he had been thinking of him.

To me, that's the crux of what we're aiming for when we talk about humanizing digital. It's baking in what people have always wanted: connection with others, to feel like they matter, and building a sense of community.

How do we replicate that basic, elemental humanity in digital?

Today, we have far more information at our fingertips than that salesperson at Marshall Field's could ever dream of. Grad Conn,[2] the former CMO of Sprinklr, told me a story that touches on the opportunity we have as marketers to bring a new level of intimacy to the things we now take for granted. As we get back into the habit of traveling in this post-COVID world, Grad explained to me:

> *I'm a platinum rewards member with Marriott, and I'm also a loyal, 30-year airline frequent flyer program member. Hotels and airlines know something about you, but they don't know the complete*

picture—they don't know what happened to you during the course of the entire day. But the data exists. One time, I had a terrible flight. Not that I would say anything about it, but I messaged them. They quickly got back to me and that made me feel somewhat good, but it was just in that moment. I still had to rebook my flights and I still had a rough day.

By the time I got to my hotel, I was not in a good mood. I was not feeling great about the experience that I had on my flight, and that had nothing to do with Marriott. Can you imagine the data that exists now, and the ability for Marriott to know that you had a bad day? It's out there. And because you're a platinum rewards member, when you check in, they could instantly create an uplifting experience by giving you a room upgrade or a day pass to the spa or some other amenity. Those connections are now possible.

So, when I say, "back to the future," that's what I mean. There have always been those consummate salespeople—such as the Marshall Field's toy department salesperson—who know how to connect and be intimate with their customers. And their managers knew how to teach and encourage other salespeople to do those things—to make it feel like they were thinking about you and making some of your problems go away. If you lived in a small town, that salesperson or shopkeeper probably knew that you ran the mill, and maybe someone was injured cutting down a tree the other day. Or that your spouse was a member of the PTA, and your daughter was on the high school basketball team. Those things were in their heads.

The most powerful computer on the planet is still the human brain, but it starts losing its ability to track individuals after 50 to 100 people. Our brains max out and it's increasingly difficult for us to remember their personal details beyond that number. But now we have the ability to get those prompts. We can use intelligent systems and pick and choose the right data to bring things together in a way that hitherto we would only have been able to do at a very limited scale maybe 150 years ago. The future is now, and it's our job to put it to work on behalf of our customers.

Obstacles to Building Empathy

Although this book digs deep into why organizations need to refocus on people and recalibrate their power sharing, making those things happen can be much easier said than done. In my experience, I have found there are a number of obstacles that often get in the way.

One such obstacle is that the structure of most organizations, whether B2B or B2C, is geared in many ways to only look at a slice of the customer. Individuals who touch the customer are only seeing a very small moment of their customers' lives or a very small part of their ongoing needs or frustrations. I go back to the example of the previously loyal Craftsman customer in Chapter 2 who stated that he would never buy anything from Sears again. He felt with great certainty that because he had spent so much money at Sears over a period of many years, and because he was in own mind as loyal as he could possibly be, somehow in the magic of technology the company would know who he was when he walked up to any touchpoint, whether it was online or in a store.

This gentleman had been a Sears customer for 15 years, and he had spent something like $20,000 in the preceding five years. At the time, however, there was just no way for Sears to track customer information with this level of granularity and then make it available to salespeople, online customer service reps, or anyone else in the company in any meaningful and timely way. He expected us to *know* him—to show him he was important to us as an individual—and he was immensely disappointed when he learned we did not. We let him down.

The problem is the difference between personalization and humanization. So, when we used to talk about being personal, we were really talking about how data and technology start to predict something. Again, not anticipating a human need, just roughly predicting. Surprisingly, even a company like Amazon doesn't—I believe—always get it right. For as much as the company knows about me from my ordering habits, I'm always bewildered that they seem to know so little. And then, even when they do know something about me, it's not the right stuff. It still feels very one dimensional, for all the data crunching that they must be doing. Although Amazon constantly works to improve their customers' experiences, most companies haven't really thought through what a great end-to-end customer experience should look like, much less implemented it.

Jeriad Zoghby is global lead of omni-channel commerce at Accenture Song. He has put a lot of thought into how data and technology can start to replicate what it means to be *personal*. Says Jeriad:

> *The question is this: How can we use data and technology to create a personal experience for consumers—not human, just personal? To get started on this problem, we used a framework we called the 4 Rs.*
>
> *The first R is recognize. If you walk into a coffee shop that you go into every day, they're going to recognize you. They know you regularly come in there. If there's somebody new behind the counter, you'd say, "Oh yeah, I come in here all the time," because the person has to ask your name. Everyone else already knows your name.*
>
> *The second R is remember—they remember you and your preferences. When I walk into the coffee shop right next to my office, the barista always says, "Same thing, right?" He knows I like a mocha with a little less milk because I prefer it to be slightly bitter. What's interesting about that is he doesn't just know what I want, he understands why I want it. That's an important nuance. He knows that it changes the flavor when there's a little less milk—the bitterness in the coffee and the chocolate comes through a little stronger.*
>
> *The third R is recommendations. Not to cross sell, not to upsell, that's just obnoxious anyway. It's to help me make decisions because what we find in life today is that we are often overwhelmed by the choices we have. Amazon might be great for transactions when you know exactly what you want, but it's a challenging place to shop otherwise because there are too many options. You feel overwhelmed, you feel less confident in your decisions, and you will often abandon the experience. Recommendations should be about making life easier. It could also be my barista saying,*

"Hey, I know you love mochas, did you see the new drink we've got now? It's made with dark chocolate which has the kind of flavor profile you like." He knows what I might care about in a new product.

The fourth R is relevance, which is when I say, "The last time I came in here, it was super busy, and somebody bumped into me and I spilled my coffee." And the barista responds, "Hey, sorry about that, it was really crazy last time you were here." Relevance is about contextual knowledge.

Some institutions—L'Oréal, for one—are now trying to aggressively build a great experience for their customers. They *want* to have those touchpoints, and they want to be able to do something with them when they're having those conversations, whether they're digital or face-to-face. Still, while organizations are starting to talk about it, very few can do it—in many cases because it seems so overwhelming. There's no roadmap for organizations to follow, and they don't actually have a complete story to tell—they have neither the beginning nor the ending. There are pieces of it scattered across the organization, but they're not stitched together into a coherent whole.

Most organizations tend to be reactive rather than proactive. Proactive in their minds translates into mass communication, mass marketing, and broadcast. But proactive in my mind—and I think Grad's and others' minds—is at a very granular level using things like automation and technology to promote the illusion that you have a greater connection. It's predict versus anticipate, which is more about the customers and where they are in the moment. At least you've made the effort, but you can't do it if you don't have all these pieces working together.

In an interview, Jeriad Zoghby told me about a company where three key systems—their recommendation engine, their testing tool, and their digital analytics platform—were definitely not working well together. He says:

It used to drive me nuts—all three had different measurement systems. They were working against one another, and they had different objectives.

One was trying to cross sell. Another was trying to engage in a conversation. And the whole goal of the testing tool was, "Hey, if I want to introduce something new that you're going to experience, how do I know it's going to work with everything else?" This is not being human. This is just trying to get data and systems to feel more like the personal coffee shop experience.

Now, put that aside for a second. The basic foundation that many companies still struggle with is how [to] not act like a technology platform and actually feel personal. Now, if I want to be human, that's different—a big leap beyond.

More often we will talk about experiences, and a lot of organizations think they can solve this by hiring chief experience officers. But if you think about it for a moment, that is at least a declaration that experience matters and that you want to bring things together under this umbrella. You might be a B2B company like Caterpillar or John Deere, and you've come to the realization that marketing needs to be part of customer service and they need to work hand in hand. And this needs to promote an overall experience that then ladders up into what we think the brand promise is and being able to manage it in a more granular, personal fashion.

The problem is that this is not enough going forward. The next frontier is fusing the human back into the overall experience, and believe me, that is not easy. Not because of the data and technology needed to pull it off, but more important, because of the mindset and organization required to be truly authentic.

Right now, we're at the point at which maybe a few companies understand that this is critically important. They're all-in, and they're striving to get there. But I believe most organizations still think that since they've devolved a lot of authority to individual operations—marketing, sales, customer care, analytics, and so on—and each one has an executive who has a very clear idea of what their parts should be—that they've done all they need to do.

I liken the situation we have right now to the Japanese film *Rashomon*, in which a particular event was described in different—and often contradictory—ways by each of the main characters who were involved in it. You never got the full picture of what actually happened until the very end of the film because everyone told the same story over and over again, but from their own unique perspective. Then finally all the threads came together. That's where we're at today—it's one thing that's structurally in the way.

I think we're also in a place where people are a little jaded. They've been told that they can accomplish some amazing marketing things—building the classic Peppers and Rogers one-to-one relationships, for example—by using all the remarkable technologies at our disposal. Build a fantastic data repository, and they will come. But in truth, it's much more difficult than just gathering gobs of data and analyzing it. The installation of a great platform isn't going to solve your complex marketing, sales, and service problems all by itself. You've got to go much deeper than that. Solving those deep problems requires rethinking your operational imperative, how you function together, where data resides, how it's distributed, how quickly it's distributed, and in what form.

Jeriad Zoghby has identified three things required to turn everyday digital experiences into something more human. As Jeriad explains:

The first thing is shifting from profiling customers to listening to them. Profiling is where you gather as much data about your customer as you can—age, gender, ZIP code, income level, and so on—and then decide what product to pitch them. In reality, profiling is not personal, it's not human. It's very cold. And, let's be honest, in this day and age, it's also to the point of being provocatively on the wrong side of public opinion. Instead of profiling, ask: "I want to know not what you do; I want to understand why you do it." The big shift is from the what to the why.

The second thing, and to me this is the most important, is the difference between prediction versus anticipation. If Uber shows up at my house before I ask for it, that's creepy—a bad experience. But if Uber understands the demand in the area, and makes the car available when I need it, that's wonderful. Giving me what I want on my own terms is a phenomenal, wonderful experience. The difference, when we start to talk about anticipation versus prediction, is who's in control? Prediction says, "As the brand, I know what you need. I've come up with all your customer journeys and now I'm going to direct you down this path." Anticipation flips the script and says to the customer, "You're in control. All I'm going to do is give you all the various options that are available and you pick whatever journey you want to be on."

The third thing is the difference between shifting from assistance to expertise. Amazon's Alexa, for example, is not expertise—it's an assistant. This is the thing with expertise. If you went to a Best Buy and you asked for help with a television sound bar, the salesperson you talked with might not have been an expert, but they knew who in their store was. They'd say, "Let me ping Kathy. She knows everything there is to know about these sound bars. I'll go get her." Expertise meant something to us because it built confidence in the decisions we made. In digital, we've lost that expertise because what we've moved to is a cost-savings and efficiency model and we've pretended that expertise came along with it. It didn't, and we need to figure out how to inject expertise into the digital realm.

There are definitely organizations that do this very well, but they tend to do it in areas outside of marketing. They have put a stake in the ground about what they are and what they're going to bring to bear as a company, and then how that's going to infuse this into every decision they make, every person they hire, every project they run. One such company is Capital One, where for the first time in financial services, they made the decision to create a company where analytics would dominate every aspect of their DNA. Their commitment was to out-analyze the competition, and to do it faster and more granularly than anyone else. They believed with tremendous certainty that this would provide them with what they needed to create new products that no one had ever thought of that would meet some very specific customer needs and demands while earning a profit.

Capital One's approach was fascinating to me. Here's an organization that has an organizing principle—top down, bottom up—where everyone who works for or with the company all have to go through a rigorous assessment of their analytic capabilities because that's their DNA. They want everyone to think that way, they select for it, and as a result they do.

And of course, if you want to find a company where design is core to their DNA, you need only look to Apple. Everyone who plays a role in the company—employees, vendors, consultants, and so on—must keep that in mind and align around this principle. They may have other duties and things to consider as they do their jobs, but they have to appreciate that they are building *solutions*, not just products, that are well-designed for people so that they can use the company's technologies effectively.

These kinds of companies are anomalies—I don't know if you could come up with a list of even 100 such organizations, which demonstrates just how hard it is. But somewhere in the history of Capital One and Apple, someone put a stake in the ground and said, "this is who we are and what we're going to stand for."

Another obstacle—although increasingly it's changed from being a fixed one to a moving one—is privacy. It's an obstacle because it's constantly changing and because social norms are constantly changing. That makes it hard for organizations to determine the best or the right way around it. But privacy is a trade-off. If I as the customer feel I am really getting value for sharing a piece of information, then I don't feel so concerned that an organization knows something about me. But if that same organization sucks up my every keystroke without providing me anything obvious in return, then I may have a real issue. It is about sharing power, and those organizations that get it and take meaningful steps to change the balance of power with their customers, employees, and wider community will have a major advantage over their competitors in riding the next wave of growth.

I believe people tend to think about privacy as an objective to overcome versus something that you need to embrace. I know a lot of companies that have made privacy an important part of what they do and their brand promise—most every company today says, "We're not going to sell products to you based on the information we gather about you—this is just for us." And then they proceed to use that information in a tone-deaf way to bombard the person with marketing offers, even though they haven't sold off the information to someone else.

Again, I think you have to put yourself in your customers' shoes and think about what privacy means to them. Many customers are okay with letting you know something about them, so long as there's a real benefit to them and so long as you stick by certain principles that they know they can count on. They expect you not to constantly change the yardstick or move the goalposts. It's amazing how much information there is available about people out in the world today, that they were quite willing to give away for free. But I think people are also starting to realize that there's a value to be had from their data, and there will probably come a day when people want to be rewarded for the information they provide, and they will want to be granted more control over it.

When, for example, my wife and I started making the move to television streaming services, we thought, "This is great. We like having control over our programming. We like watching the shows we want when we want. We like having more granular control over what we pay." There were also businesses running ads in these streaming services, which was fine with us—we didn't disagree with that. In those early days, we were given the opportunity as customers to say, "I don't like that ad," and the idea was that the ad would be pulled from our streams and they would show us a different one. The thought was that someone or something was taking a look at the kinds of things we didn't want to see, which we were quite willing to tell them. We actually looked forward to getting advertisements that were more relevant to us.

Truth is, that never happened.

Even when you told them the five things you were most interested in, none of those ads ever showed up on the streaming service. It struck me as the most bizarre thing I could imagine. In this world in which we live, we have the ability to tell advertisers the things we're most interested in, and the adjacent things we would be open to hearing more about. How much more impactful would it be if marketers actually followed through on that ability? The impact would be massive, but at least in the case of the streaming service my wife and I were using, someone clearly made the decision that the approach wasn't working for them, and so they took it away from their customers.

Maybe it's naivety on my part because I don't buy ads every day, but if you were able to say, "Here's my audience, and here's how I've segmented them, and here are the things they are really, really interested in, then approximately 10 percent of them would be very interested in this kind of luxury vehicle and those types of snack foods and this type of a getaway vacation," (because—wait for it—they told us). And that would seem to be a very powerful competitive advantage to me.

If we didn't have to sell everything and couch everything in terms of cost per thousand (CPM), but instead something came up with a measure that was more about cost per impact (CPI), I believe that would change the game. The value of those impressions should go way up because they're more targeted. But it's very hard to put something like this in place because, as hard as it is for me to understand why, it's considered to be an extremely radical idea.

How Should We Frame the Problem?

I think part of the problem is that when we're hunkered down doing our jobs, nose to the grindstone, we simply forget to be human. I can't count how many meetings I've been in where someone says something like, "And if we did this, then people would do that." My first thought is to ask them, "But would *you* want to do this? Would you react to that well?" If we could use facial recognition as someone enters a grocery store to see that someone is unhappy, and do a quick scan of their previous purchases to discover they have a hemorrhoidal condition, should we shoot them a text message with an offer for half off Preparation H?

The answer is probably not, because we didn't first take the time to walk a mile in that person's shoes, and we didn't think about the process empathetically.

I believe that we have to get away from the idea that people are audiences to be marketed to and instead focus on how to forge real connections with our customers. Part of that's going to happen through automation, part through one-to-one, and part through face-to-face. But it's all got to feel the same when the customer experiences it.

What's key, I think, to this transformation is changing the mindset. It's putting yourself in that person's shoes, in that audience's shoes—as difficult as that may sound—and getting away from traditional segmentation. That old-school approach might have worked to some degree in the past, but it's not going to get us where we want to go in the twenty-first century. Segments aren't static—people's wants and needs change. Context is everything.

So how do you build the experiential part of your organization around context, and how then do you go back to the future?

My suggestion? Organize your entire organization around these kinds of basic principles: Anyone who has *any* contact with *any* customer has got to think like a marketer, a salesperson, and a customer service rep, because those touchpoints are the experiences that, in the end, tell you what your brand is. You don't *tell* people what your brand is anymore—that flavor of brand promise is dead, in my view.

I don't buy suits often, but I did have to buy a few recently when my wife said to me one day, "I don't like the suits you have." Admittedly, they were totally old fashioned (the pants had pleats and the jackets three-buttons), but I countered that they were very high quality, and no one cares about the pleats anyway. But my wife stuck to a consistent message and hit me with this kicker: "I think they make you look old."

That was all she had to say, and with that we went shopping together one weekend. I hadn't gone suit shopping for about 10 years, and after some fits and starts we walked into a Hugo Boss store. They were having a sale, so it didn't take too much persuading.

The salesperson who helped us was brilliant. First, he plied me with alcohol before we even started looking—nothing gets a customer limbered up to shop faster than a whiskey. Then he sat down and listened to me and my wife like a marriage counselor peeling back the core of a long-buried friction. "Tell me what you both like and are hoping to accomplish today," he asked.

After he quickly processed our answers in his mind, the salesperson proceeded to bring suits that he thought would address our individual and joint objectives. Brilliantly, he would occasionally bring something out he knew both of us would instantly dislike just to get us both on the same side. Eventually, I found myself being fitted for two suits (primary because they ticked *my* boxes for classic cut, value, and quality along with my wife's conclusion that they made me look young and hot rather than old and stodgy.

To his credit, the salesperson sensed that I was still kind of clinging to my old suits—like old friends I was secretly betraying. So, in a final *coup de grâce*, he came back to us after speaking with the tailor. "I hear you would really like to hold on to those old suits—it sounds like they are good quality. I spoke with the tailor who I have worked with for many years, I'll give you his number, he can do amazing things with old suits. He'll come to your house, recut these suits to be more modern—more fitted, no more pleats or cuffs—and you'll have new suits that will fit like your wife wants." And sure enough, he did.

The Hugo Boss salesperson made the sale because he listened, he had expertise, and he had passion to go beyond what he had in the shop. He essentially reprised *The Miracle on 34th Street*: I don't have that here, but I know people who can do it for you and they're really good. You're going to be very happy, and that's a complete contrast to our usual experiences as consumers.

To underscore this tension between assistance versus expertise, it's more common to be frustrated as a customer when you need something that isn't on the menu. Every time you call an 800 number, and you need help—perhaps urgently, for example, when you've lost your credit card—you first have to go through the automated phone system which may or may not know what the hell you're talking about. It asks the same questions over and over, or tries to get you to conform to its rules and programmatic parameters: "Can you say that a different way?" The system should be making it easier for *me*, not the other way around.

Jeriad Zoghby put it a different way. He was in Vegas some years ago and was introduced to Wayne Newton after a show. Wayne was a wonderful guy—very warm and personable. Wayne told Jeriad a story from when he was a couple years into his Vegas career and starting to see some success. One night, Wayne was sick and not feeling well, but he still had a show to do. He asked one of the singers who'd been around for a while, "Should I tell the audience that I'm a bit under the weather?"

"Dude," the singer responded, "they don't come to hear your problems. They come to forget their own. Your job is to help them forget their own problems, not for you to share yours!"

What a powerful learning. If all organizations just had this mindset—that their job is to make a customer's experience a good one and to solve their issues, rather than add to them—how loyal do you think they would be, even if you didn't have the latest and greatest product or service?

We've all experienced the maddening situation of calling some company's customer service line seeking their help with a problem. After navigating their voice response phone tree, you finally—after 10 or more minutes—get through to a real person and explain your situation. "Oh, that's a different department. Hold on while I forward your call." As often as not, when that hand-off is made, you hear a click, and the line goes silent—another call lost. Instead of solving your problem, they've given you another of their own.

Alexa and other automated assistants do not provide expertise because expertise asks questions. The very first thing the salesperson at Hugo Boss did (after he plied me with whiskey) was to ask my wife and me some very pointed questions that would enable him to provide the kind of suit choices that would tick our boxes. He didn't just drag out some suits and ties and ask, "What about this suit? What about this one?" Experts ask really good questions, and above all they have passion—it shows.

Your brand promise is the ante, and it's only as good as how your customers perceive you. Are you living up to that basic promise—across every channel, every customer touchpoint, every time? Remember: your brand is only as healthy as your weakest link. If I have a great online ordering experience with Target, but I walk into my local Target store to pick up my order and the person who rings me up is grumpy or won't help me find my order, that's your brand. It's my last impression of who you are. The lowest common denominator is going to cloud a person's perception of what that brand is and whether they're going to come back or recommend friends or family going there.

There's an old myth based on a 1970s study commissioned by Coca-Cola that every unhappy customer tells 9–10 other people about their negative experience with a brand. Whether or not that statistic is actually true (and it is probably way higher in this day and age), it's clear that social media has greatly amplified customers' ability to share their brand stories—good and bad—with the rest of the world. More than a decade ago, a guitarist, Dave Carroll, was upset that United Airlines customer service reps repeatedly refused to compensate him for $1,200 in damage to his Taylor acoustic guitar that occurred when the airline's baggage handlers tossed it to the ground. Said a very frustrated Carroll:

> *At that moment it occurred to me that I had been fighting a losing battle all this time and that fighting over this at all was a waste of time. The system is designed to frustrate affected customers into giving up their claims ... but I realized then that as a songwriter and traveling musician I wasn't without options.*[3]

Those options included writing a song about his experience ("United Breaks Guitars") and posting a humorous video to YouTube set to his music, then sending a message to his 400 Facebook followers asking them to watch it. And watch it they did. Just four days after the video was posted, it hit 1 million views and attracted widespread attention in social and traditional media—giving United Airlines a major PR black eye that caused the company much pain for months. Some media reports even put the blame for a 10 percent dip in the company's market value on all the negative publicity.[4]

But Carroll—whose video was eventually viewed more than 20 million times—believes that his experience had an impact on more than just United Airlines. He explained:

> *"United Breaks Guitars" was an early sign that in this new digital world, one customer can affect the profitability of the world's biggest brands on a budget of, in my case, $150. Companies now are listening much more closely than they ever did before, consumers are feeling more empowered, and every customer can have a voice ... even if he or she can't sing.*[5]

When someone posts about their negative customer service experiences on social media, particularly someone who is an influencer with a large following (think the Kardashians, Cristiano Ronaldo, Taylor Swift, Justin Bieber, and so on), it has the potential to quickly turn into a feeding frenzy. It pokes the bear, and everybody who has had a similar experience weighs in with their own negative stories.

Let's be fair. We all have bad days, and so do companies and the people who work for and with them. But it's so easy now to reach so many people so quickly with a message that you did not approve and have no control over. You might think that you control the story, but the reality today is that you really don't. Traditional PR is nowhere near as effective as it once was, not in this new world of social media.

Again, it comes down to redressing the power imbalance by sharing power and focusing on the value exchange and the outcomes, not on the process. Remember to walk a mile in the customer's shoes (at all levels) and think like a shopkeeper, anticipating rather than trying to predict a customer's every move. But beyond that, it's building a sense of real community so that your customers know that you've got their backs. They feel that they have given *you* something—their loyalty, their trust, their dollars—now you need to give something back in return, over and above the norm. You need to constantly reach out to them and ask, "What else can I do for you?" or "This is where you could save some real money," or "How can I help you today in a way that's meaningful?"

Ultimately, the problem solution is within the *experience*— spending time figuring out what the best customer experience should be end to end, no matter where that road leads you. Even if it leads you outside of marketing, even if it leads you beyond customer care, wherever it might take you. That's the game you need to play. Constantly ask yourself, "How do I deliver a better experience and what are the moments that matter for my customer? And if the moments that matter are not being delivered to our customers, how do we fix that?"

The ball is in your court. Confront this issue head on right now instead of waiting for it to be flagged in some quarterly or monthly report. If something's broken, you can't wait until you've already alienated 1,500 or 10,000 people or maybe more. Why wait? Why not figure out how to do this more elastically right now?

You can and you should.

The organizing principle is experience first—the value then comes out of that. What is the value of those experiences and how do I make sure that I prioritize the things that are going to drive the most value—first for my customer first, and also for us as an organization?

Next, how do I enable that—people, processes, technologies, and data? Each one of those key players has to be aligned in a way that you normally wouldn't do. You normally wouldn't say, "Here's the experience I want to produce and here are all the things I have to change in my organization to make that work." But that's what I think truly long-lived and flexible companies are going to be doing more and more, because they're going to want to act like a nation of shopkeepers. It's going to be, "I didn't stock that jar of jam, but I'm going to get it for you—I'll have it here in the next 48 hours. I'll send you a message as soon as it's available." That level of flexibility is currently missing, and the organizing principle around experience ferrets it out very quickly.

What Do Customers Really Want?

We're all customers, and we know what we want. So figuring out what customers want shouldn't be any great mystery. Right here right now, we have the ability to listen in to what our customers are telling us on a variety of different platforms, gathering intelligence all along the way. We can do this *en masse*, we can do this in small groups, we can do this at the local level. And it is because we have access to data and technology that can make these experiences a reality at scale that we are poised to ride the next great wave of invention and growth, if only we stop and realign to what is most important—people.

In my view, customer research should have long ago made the pivot to modern channels, but the good news is it's not too late. We can continuously look at these touchpoints and mine them in real time, using automation to help.

Customers, us included, are telling organizations what they want. Just 20 or 30 years ago, we might not have had a clue. You had to get people into a focus group in some darkened room with stale M&Ms someplace and ask them questions point blank. And even then, you had to extrapolate what they were really telling you because it was just a small sample.

Today, we're sitting on an almost infinite stack of behavioral data, quantitative and qualitative information, and unstructured conversations that provide us with a hint at consumer sentiment, that give us a hint at the trajectory of their demand before it arrives, and that give us a sense of what's going right and what's going wrong. I have to think that if we were all following this prescription, there would be a lot more organizations much more closely attuned to customer demand than there are today. It still seems like a black box for many organizations.

In previous chapters, I've talked about the power of knowing three things about your most valuable customers that your competitors do not know. If you could name those three things, your company would be healthy, because you'd be ahead of the game; you would build closer relationships with your customers, you would solve their problems and address their needs proactively, and you would retain them—like the community of loyal Craftsman tool fans that we built at Sears, possibly for life.

6

The Six Pillars of Purpose-Driven Experience

As brands strive for differentiation, relevance, and growth, a clear pur-
pose brought to life in compelling ways is often the difference between
success and failure.

—Afdhel Aziz

A lot of organizations say that they stand for something—
sustainability, diversity, conquering a disease, curing some
social ill, or any number of other things to fill in the blank—but
in many cases, the stand they're taking is actually quite superfi-
cial. They make a big, public splash with their chosen cause—
sending out press releases, putting videos on their website, filling
their social channels with announcements and proclamations—
but they don't follow through with real action. It's theater
of purpose.

So, why bother? They do all this and more because they
know that people—customers, customers-to-be—care about the
values of the companies with which they do business. They want
to buy products and services from companies that share the same
values they do. And they don't just take a company's word for it.
Today, more than ever before, consumers are checking to make
sure brands are following through on their promises.

And employees and job candidates are checking those brands too. They're going to look at where you stand on these things and what exactly you've actually done in support of those stands. And they're going to make decisions based on that because they see companies as having an important role and responsibility in society beyond just providing products or services.

There has been a great deal of research conducted recently on purpose-driven experience and the importance of purpose being embedded in the foundation of corporate values and business practices. In its fourteenth annual Accenture Strategy Global Consumer Pulse Research, titled "From Me to We: The Rise of the Purpose-led Brand," Accenture surveyed 30,000 global consumers to better understand their expectations around purpose. What it found was revealing.

The study found that 63 percent of consumers are buying goods and services from companies that reflect their personal values and beliefs, and 62 percent of consumers want companies to take a stand on social, cultural, environmental, and political issues close to their hearts. In addition, 62 percent of consumers say that their purchasing decisions are influenced by a company's ethical values and authenticity; 74 percent want transparency into how companies source their products, ensure safe working conditions, and their stance on important issues; and 47 percent report that they have stopped doing business with a company as a result of its actions.[1]

Said Bill Theofilou, senior managing director at Accenture Strategy:

Purpose is more than companies simply responding to issues of the day. It's about having a genuine and meaningful commitment to important principles that consumers care about—such as health and well-being, natural ingredients, environmental sustainability and family connections—which inform every business decision. Many companies have neglected to convey purpose due to complacency, lethargy, or the fear of polarizing people, which has allowed smaller players to rise.[2]

For much of the course of human history, there have been powerful institutions that people looked to for guidance and for something to believe in, for good and for bad. For the most part, these institutions were military, governmental, or religious. In just one example, the Roman Catholic Church wielded considerable power for centuries, and millions of people invested their trust, loyalty, and allegiance in its leaders. They aligned with the beliefs and values of the church, and sometimes they put their lives on the line to uphold them, whether for perceived good or sometimes unforeseen bad. Regardless of the outcomes, purpose galvanized adherents and remains a powerful adhesive because it springs from the community.

Business and commerce have existed for almost as long as there have been people—the oldest company in the world is said to be a hot spring hotel called Nishiyama Onsen Keiunkan in Japan, which opened in 705 and has been continuously operated by the same family for many generations.[3] But it wasn't until the latter part of the twentieth century and early in the twenty-first century when large corporations and conglomerates emerged—in many ways taking the place of the institutions that people once believed in and pledged their allegiance to. Ford, Coca-Cola, IBM—you name it. Each of these brands generated the kind of trust, loyalty, and allegiance that the military, governmental, and religious institutions held before them.

Today, you can almost chart the connection between customer engagement and the importance of where companies stand on certain issues.

Thirty years or more ago, if there was a big, negative event involving a business—an oil company spilling millions of gallons of crude over a pristine shoreline, or a cigarette company being accused of selling products that caused cancer in its customers—it seemed isolated, insulated, a one-off. But I believe the first turn of that came full circle when governments got more involved in things like regulating the amount of lead in products, including paint and gasoline. Up until that point, companies could add lead to their products to their heart's content, and people liked that just fine because lead made their paint dry faster and last longer while making their car engines run smoother. They told us it was better, and we tended to accept the narrative. We didn't have any other information to contradict the assertions.

Eventually, some more maverick researchers began to question the status quo, sometimes by accident in the quest to support some of those assertions or because they were looking at seemingly unrelated phenomenon. Researchers such as Clair Patterson proved that lead was everywhere and poisoning us all. Herbert Needleman proved that the lead-containing paint that children were peeling off the walls of their homes and eating was causing neurological damage. They showed that the lead in gasoline was ending up dispersed in the environment—resulting in serious, negative health outcomes for everyone exposed to it. Even so, it took several decades for this information to push its way into the public psyche sufficiently enough to compel regulators to require companies to make a change.

That is no longer the case. With always-on television news and social channels such as Twitter, Facebook, Instagram, TikTok, and more, customers are able to engage with the world directly and immediately. So, now, when a brand has a big, negative event—or even a small one—it's like pouring gasoline on a fire because people all across the globe have instant access to this information. And chances are, they will react.

On one hand, this is a good thing because it increases transparency and gives consumers agency. Companies are compelled to reveal the truth about what's really going on within their four walls. But on the other hand, it often puts companies at a distinct disadvantage because not only are they unable to control the narrative, sometimes the information that's being presented could be considered unfair and completely wrong. It's a double-edged sword.

Companies today are considered to have special responsibilities as these large and powerful entities that people declare their allegiance to. People expect these organizations to behave in a certain way that aligns with their own values. And if they don't, companies' feet will be held to the fire based on what they say they'll do, or more important, what they actually follow through on. Now, the question is this: What are these institutions really doing to promote a cause, whether that's diversity, gender equality, environmental responsibility, and so forth and so on? It's important to answer this question because I don't expect that this focus on the part of consumers is going to decrease anytime soon. In fact, I'm convinced it will continue to be even more critical going forward.

Gene Cornfield is managing director and global lead, Digital/Customer Experience Transformation, for Accenture Song. Gene explains that there are three levels of purpose—company, brand, and customer—and that companies can drive growth and other metrics by delivering experiences that are aligned with these three levels. Says Gene:

> *The first level is big-P purpose—company purpose. What is the company's role in the world? The second level is medium-P purpose, or brand purpose—what's the company's role in the lives of its customers? But most important, almost counterintuitively, is small-P purpose—customer purpose. What is the universe of things your customers are trying to achieve? That's what comprises your customer purpose portfolio. And it's more important to deeply understand your customer's purpose portfolio than your own product portfolio. Because ultimately, when people are buying, they're not buying your what, they're solving for their why, which is their purpose.*

When we talk about purpose-driven experience, or purpose-driven anything, it's not sufficient to just pick a purpose and get behind it. You've almost got to think like you're running a small country or a government. If you're a company board, you've got to be very concerned about how you are being perceived by your customers—your most valuable customers in particular—and how you manage that relationship in terms of being transparent and proactive while showing people what you're actually doing in the community, but being very consistent about it. It's not sufficient to say, "We planted a few trees, aren't we great?" You've got to be in a position to say, "We've actually done this. We believe in this. We want you to get involved with us if you can. Because we recognize as an institution that we have a higher-order responsibility than just to our shareholder profitability on Wall Street."

But there's danger here too. People support or flee from organizations based on what they perceive them to be actually doing and standing for. Patagonia makes no bones about its core values, which include doing less harm and doing more good, and using business to protect nature.[4] Similarly, Chick-fil-A's corporate purpose is clear and unequivocal: "To glorify God by being a faithful steward of all that is entrusted to us. To have a positive influence on all who come in contact with Chick-fil-A."[5] These companies attract or repel customers, employees, investors, and others in no small part because of the values they embrace.

Now more than ever, it's harder to tread a fine line where you're not likely to offend anyone. In fact, you're very likely to offend someone based on what you say, do, or believe in, or what your standard is. But I also think it's an opportunity to not just get people's dander up or find yourself in a sticky wicket because you're caught between two worlds, and you can't figure out how to satisfy anybody. There's also an opportunity here for organizations to be clear about what they stand for through a purpose-driven strategy. And there are things you can stand for that I believe everyone can get behind—higher-order elements such as fairness and transparency and being a good steward of the world.

Peter Smith is global managing director, Experience & Marketing AI at Accenture. In an interview, Peter described what consumers are looking for in their brands today:

> *Customers today are looking to brands to contribute to solving some of society's problems. They want to be treated like a person and not a number. They want brands to take stances on issues such as social justice. And they're voting with their pocketbooks. And so, all these trends tell me one big thing: that customers want greater humanity from the businesses and brands that serve them. And you can see this manifesting in the best brands out there over the course of the last 10 years or so.*
>
> *There's the example of Nike's iconic Colin Kaepernick ad from 2018, which won all kinds of awards. If you think about what Nike was selling in the ad, it wasn't shoes. They didn't say why you should buy Nike versus Adidas for the athletic performance gains you might get. Nike was selling its values. Steve Jobs once said that you have a customer's attention for a very limited amount of time, so you don't sell them on your product, you sell them on your values.*
>
> *I think a lot of brands since the rise of Apple have taken that to heart. They really think about what the brand's values are, how they project them into the world, and how they embody them in terms of how they interact and engage with their customers. And the interesting thing is that as we've observed in our Business of Experience report, companies building in this more human feature are far more profitable than others in their peer sets.*

You don't have to use the buzzwords that cause people consternation to take a stand for things that are important to your organization, your people, and yourself. Instead of tackling the big, hairy, hot-button issues of the day that no one feels like they can control or influence, you can simply say, for example, "We believe in a world where everyone gets a fair shake, and we work together to make things better. Here's exactly what we're doing to help make the world a better place, and here's the size of our programs."

These values can then cascade into how you deal with your customers themselves. You can say, "We believe in that same fair shake for our customers. And here's our customer Bill of Rights. No one's telling us we have to do this; we just think it's the right thing to do. So, join with us to make the world a better place."

Whatever you tell your customers you believe in, ultimately, your goal is to make sure they are happy with the products or services that they've contracted for and purchased. You want to make sure your customers understand what you do with their data, in a simple, easy-to-understand way. You should never send them off to read the fine print your legal department threw together and buried deep in your website, where few of your customers will find it much less actually read it. There are plenty of examples of organizations that do that today.

How you get your purpose into an organization and how you get people to align with it is critically important for it to become something that's real—more than just heartwarming words and photos splashed across your website. And this takes an effort that is both bottoms up and top down. It doesn't work if you have just one or the other, if you can't get people behind the values that comprise and animate your purpose. It's hard for a CEO who may believe in certain things to get people behind her if she doesn't clearly and repeatedly explain the organization's purpose. And vice versa. If there's grassroots support for a purpose, but the organization's leadership isn't saying, "Yes, we should support this—this is good," it will quickly fade.

It's hard to get behind something if you're an employee and you don't see where all this is going. So often, the well-meaning initiatives of leaders can still turn into platitudes and hollow promises, which ultimately ignore the grassroots needs of an organization and its customers. And it's hard for leaders who must navigate all these issues on a day-to-day basis. Where does purpose fit into the overall hierarchy of what's most important to manage and run a company in the twenty-first century?

I'm a bit of Trekkie (a fan of the Star Trek universe, for the uninitiated). I like to think that the creator of that universe, Gene Roddenberry, had had a pretty good handle on where we should go as a society. Not necessarily where we are, but where we should go. I sometimes find myself looking for leadership examples in episodes of the original *Star Trek* television and film series as well as *The Next Generation*. These shows and films celebrate the triumph of good over evil, and I think for leaders, the message is that whatever you do in the end, hopefully the decisions you make will be informed by doing the right thing. It might not be the *easy* thing. It might not be the *expedient* thing. But it's the *right* thing. And that's probably one of the hardest things for leaders to navigate given their competing and often unaligned stakeholders and interests.

This is where the rubber hits the road. Companies have always been ultimately focused on the bottom line, and they all have to be focused there to a certain degree. The simple fact is that a company must make money to stay in business. It can be doing the greatest good in the world, but if the business is not sustainable—if it doesn't generate enough revenue to sustain operations, or enough profit to scale and grow—then it will ultimately suffer, and perhaps even fail. Businesses aren't social organizations in the strictest sense, nor are they community-based nonprofits, though they can undoubtedly do much good when they focus their resources on achieving some social good at the intersection of social and business purpose.

But I find that, if you can do this sort of thing—if you can get behind it in the right way—then I think it does go to the bottom line. If you can get your employees behind the organization and where it's going as a brand vision from a business perspective, that's one thing. But if you can also parlay that and say, "This is a great place to be, and here's why." You must demonstrate that every day. If you say, "I reward people for being transparent and honest and caring about others," then you have to reward people for doing that. And if you're able to do that and do it consistently, it pays dividends. You will have more highly qualified and talented people who are more loyal, who stay with your organization longer, who are more engaged in their jobs, and who want to provide great experiences for your customers.

According to a recent U.S. Bureau of Labor survey, younger baby boomers (born from 1957 through 1964) had an average of 12.4 jobs during the ages of 18 to 54—or a new job about every three years.[6] And according to a study recently released by the IBM Institute for Business Value, 1 in 5 employees voluntarily changed employers in 2020, with 33 percent of Gen Z and 25 percent of Millennials among the job hoppers. Here are the top three reasons cited by study respondents for changing employers (the second is particularly noteworthy):

1. I needed more flexibility in my schedule or work location (32 percent)
2. I wanted to find more purposeful, meaningful work (27 percent)
3. I needed more benefits and support for my well-being (26 percent)

Fifth on the list were people who changed employers because they wanted a salary increase or promotion (25 percent).[7] As you can clearly see, purpose is a key determinant of whether employees stick with an employer or leave for greener grass. And it's not just regular workers who are leaving their jobs behind. Pressure is so high in the C-suite that either they leave or they get asked to leave because of performance.

Here's the thing though: the cost of employee turnover is astronomical. The cost to recruit and train a single employee is analogous to the cost of recruiting a new customer. According to Work Institute, the cost of a departing employee to an organization ranges from 33 percent to 200 percent of the employee's annual salary.[8] This makes keeping good employees particularly important. Just as it's far less expensive to retain customers than it is to replace lost ones, it is far less expensive to retain employees than it is to replace them. And this is where we're going wrong.

The free-market concept for employees is great, but it's also a double-edged sword that leads us to a situation in which we are challenged to retain talent. And when you can't retain talent, that hits you at the core of your business and it also hits you in your ability to innovate, which increasingly requires a shorter and shorter time frame. And trust (or lack thereof) is increasingly a major theme. Those companies that can build trust (through commitment to well-being, flexibility, empowerment, transparency, and communicating authentic purpose that everyone can get behind) are more likely the organizations that are most able to hold onto their talent. The value you unlock once you start retaining your people versus shifting gears every year and a half is tremendous. And it's just as true of customers as it is of employees.

This is a simple Bill of Rights for customers, employees, and key stakeholders:

- We will establish and maintain trust by being clear, honest, and transparent in our communications with customers and employees.
- We will recognize who our customers and employees are and understand what is important to them.
- We will treat our customers and employees as unique individuals (treat them they we would like to be treated).
- Our customers and employees have a right to understand and control the data collected about them.
- We will work to build experiences that anticipate our customer and employee needs based on listening to them.
- We will run our business based on customer and employee metrics that drive meaningful and mutual benefit.
- We will ensure customers and employees understand and align with our organization's core purpose.

How do we accomplish this? With the six pillars.

Personalized Care and Recognition

To me, having more personalized interactions and experiences is table stakes. It's what you need to do to recognize someone as who they are. And nothing is more frustrating to us as customers or employees as when a brand or employer thinks of us as just another number, another sale—some faceless person who is like everyone else.

The stories in this book consistently echo this desire that people want to feel like they matter. It's a tremendously powerful emotional need, built deep within our human DNA as social creatures, because, as social creatures, if we don't matter, we're alone—by ourselves. And we're not designed to be by ourselves.

So walking into a store and having someone recognize your face and know you as a loyal customer makes you feel good. And when that someone who recognizes you goes even further and demonstrates they've been thinking about you, even when you're not there in the store, that makes you feel even better. This is like the Marshall Field' salesman who thought about my father when a product arrived that he thought my siblings and I would like. Those things that we used to take for granted when we were a nation of shopkeepers, and when people could keep stuff straight in their heads, have now been expanded.

What can we do with digital to mirror that same experience? What can we do when someone comes to the website? There are so few sites that recognize customers until they've logged in. And in many websites, after you've logged in, nothing happens. You're directed to a landing page and there you sit— waiting for something to happen. I think this is where there is a big opportunity for brands to show their customer that they recognize them and then begin to provide them with personalized experiences.

Today we have the technology that can start assembling conversations in a way that's meaningful, that addresses the person in a personal way. It can be something simple like starting a conversation the minute you log in to say, "Hello, Rob. I'm glad you're back. It's been a while. What can I do for you today?" And then serving up some options of things based on the customer's behavior or interests or any number of other parameters. Is there something you want to reorder or is there something new you want to look at? Then guide the customer through that without being obtrusive or in the way. That, I believe, is going to be the next frontier.

It's not just, "We'll pop in an interstitial ad"; it's "What can we do throughout the journey that someone has, to help them along—up to and including helping them out with something they're about to buy?" Here's an example. I was recently online to find and buy smoke detectors for our new house. And you'd think it would be a simple process to go on a site, consider the different brands available, then make your buying decision based on price. But that wasn't the case for me, and I suspect it's not for many potential buyers of smoke detectors. The thing is, it's one of those things that you don't pay a ton of attention to, but when you need it, you want to make sure it's there and that it works the way it's supposed to.

I was personally looking for a smoke detector that also had the ability to detect carbon monoxide, and I wanted it to be hardwired into my home's electrical system with battery backup. In addition, I wanted a detector that could be also connect with my home security system. As I quickly found out, it is incredibly hard to find the specific product you're looking for when you try to take that path. It's easy to find smoke detectors, no problem. But it's extremely difficult as a consumer to find smoke detectors that are hardwired, that are smart and talk to one another via Wi-Fi, that connect with a home security system, and that have a CO detector embedded in them. Why is that the case, especially today when we have so much data and technology at our fingertips?

There are *tons* of examples of companies personalizing the experience in B2B, where customers expect a significant degree of high touch or where they want to have some guided suggestions or a way to have their questions answered directly. Right now, that's very doable, but I don't see many companies doing it in the B2C arena. It makes me wonder whether it's because organizations and brands don't see the value, or if they think it's just too hard to do. Do they think there's no need to bother since customers are buying their products anyway?

The idea of personalized care and recognition is recognizing someone for who they are—the first of Jeriad Zoghby's 4 Rs from Chapter 5. Not being too clever, but actually being helpful when you do recognize them, and going beyond a simplistic "people who bought this also bought that" presentation of buying options. We're not in the 1990s—we are *way* beyond that. It should be possible to see the buying process or the service process as something that is a recognized journey during which the information that customers share with you goes to their profiles, which in turn generates the next interaction.

Jeriad told me about a test his team ran for a national grocery chain. They built a proof-of-concept tool that, as a customer shopped, would recognize the product they picked up and would make suggestions in real time based on what the customer already shared about their diet, taste profiles, and other preferences. If, for example, their diet was gluten free, the tool would warn that a product they picked up had gluten in it. It would then suggest other, gluten-free products they could buy instead. It put power back in the customers' hands; they owned the data, and the grocery store just managed and facilitated it. The customer could change their preferences in the tool anytime they wanted to. And every time the preferences were changed by the customer, the store was dynamically re-curated for them.

This is what we automatically do in our heads with humans. But we are singularly incapable, it seems, to mirror that in our digital interactions. It should not be that way. It should be possible to think about the context of someone's interaction as much as just who they are. In fact, I know that it is.

There are plenty of technologies, right here and now. They're not perfect yet, but that doesn't matter. You can have preemptive automated conversations with people. When you log into your bank account, the first thing that you should be able to do is get to where you need to go very quickly. But if you look at most websites for financial institutions, they're not the easiest to navigate. Maybe your checking account pops up on top, but there are just so many different ways to get lost, so many different ways to get confused, so many rabbit holes to fall into. The result is frustrating for customers. We need to be more visual about the experiences our customers and employees live through to understand what to fix. Peter Smith provided me with a particularly frustrating experience he had with a large telecommunications company:

> I was presenting on a call to about 450 people. I had reached my crescendo slide and my internet cut out. It was very frustrating. Fortunately, I have a good boss who knows what I do. She jumped in and was able to fill in the blanks for me, but I was enraged. It was one of my first presentations about what we're working on in front of a large audience. And then, literally within 30 minutes after my internet cut out, I got a marketing promotion on my phone from the same company to sign up for a television streaming service. It made me want to throw my phone out the window.
>
> "How tone deaf can you be?" I thought to myself. The company knew I was experiencing an outage. In fact, they probably also knew that I was broadcasting to a large audience because I was hitting the team's IP addresses. They could look at the traffic and understand what I was doing. But instead of that, they sent me a promotion. They were also tone deaf because I don't even have a television streaming device from them.
>
> So, the organization wasn't doing the basic thing of understanding the context of me as a customer when they sent me that promotion. Current AI technology can look at the entire customer base and all my customer records and say, "Okay, we want to send Peter a promotion. But we recognize that he just had an internet outage. Let's apologize for it. Let's make it contextual to his experience."

And they could go one step further, noting that my kids are streaming a lot of Pokémon these days and there's a new Pokémon movie coming out on HBO Max. They could create the linkage and send me a personalized email based on that. AI can do that today, but templatized and rules-based email marketing cannot.

So, why not think about it empathetically from the customer point of view? In the banking example, what's the typical reason this particular individual visits our site? If it's simply to look at their checking account balance, then let's help them do that. If it's to track their investments, then let's help them do that. Let's not be in the way, but let's try to get them to where they need to be as fast as possible. That technology exists today, and it can be used to great advantage to provide personalized care and recognition to customers.

Trust and Transparency

Trust and transparency go to the fundamental question of whether you see the connection you have with a customer or an employee as something that is truly a relationship or something that is simply mechanical. Some companies are very mechanical—they aren't looking for a relationship and that's fine. But I think sometimes we overengineer what we mean by *relationship*.

In truth, having a relationship with customers or employees doesn't mean that you've got to be thinking about them 24/7 or that they have to be the best of friends with your particular brand. For me, relationships are about building trust through personalized care and recognition. That A, you recognize me; B, you care; and C, you're willing to invest a little bit of time to get to know me a little bit better. That's how you gain my trust.

The biggest trust issue that brands constantly deal with today is that everyone knows you're collecting information on them. Every second of every day, every interaction that we have, every keystroke, every mouse click, every swipe—information is being gleaned about us and our behavior and our intent, the things that frustrate us and the things that make us happy. The real questions are: Do you need all that information? And if you're collecting it, what are you doing with it that's really meaningful? Because the expectation that you're going to do something meaningful for me as a customer or employee has grown exponentially with the amount of data that's being collected.

You might recall the example I cited in another chapter about the early days of streaming where they would ask questions about your preferences to create a better experience for the consumer. I actually liked that approach to gathering data from customers and then doing something meaningful with it. When brands send me ads for things I'm not interested in, they're wasting their money and my time—and their advertisers' ad budgets. So why aren't brands collecting things that stick with me as a customer in a way that is more tailored to the things I'm interested in? When that's the case, I don't have any trouble volunteering and giving brands this information when I know they're going to use it for something that's in my benefit, more specifically, to serve me ads for things I'm actually interested in. It makes my experience more pleasurable, more efficient, and more relevant—all good things for me, the consumer.

Sure, if someone likes a particular brand of car, or a particular type of food, you might try to persuade them to try something else, but it would be a lot smarter to first gain an understanding of what someone's preferences are, then send ads their way that hit those preferences directly. Otherwise, the rest of the stuff is noise. If I have expressed an interest in Porsches, I might be interested to see an ad for the hot new Audi that was just released. And again, in this day and age, we have the technology to do that. It's not rocket science.

When people sign up for an account, you could ask them to tell you the things they're really interested in. Alternatively, you could ask them as they work their way through your site. Give them numerous opportunities to say, "I'm not interested in this thing, so don't show me anything like that again, but I *am* interested in these five things—you can send me those all day long and I'll look at them, click on them, and do something with them." People are quite smart when it comes down to the things that they're interested in. So why not give them the things they're interested in?

The number one thing that underscores trust is that people feel that they've been heard. When customers tell you what they're interested in, but you keep coming at them with things they're not interested in, that erodes trust. It makes customers think that they're just an algorithm and that you don't know who they are, and you don't care. In addition, when you send people things they aren't interested in, it makes their lives more difficult. They don't want to have to unfollow you or remove themselves from your email list, but if you keep hitting them with things they don't want, you may encourage them to do just that.

Brands today have to make some tough choices about where they stand on certain things, whereas 50, 40, 30, 20, even 10 years ago they didn't have to do that nearly as much. People want to know where the companies they buy products and services stand, and they want to see what these companies are actually doing. And it's not just whether you're fulfilling your brand promise. Do you deliver your orders on time? Do you stand by the quality of your merchandise or your services? That's all good, but that's the bare minimum. If you don't do that, you don't even have the right to hang out a shingle.

But if you say your company is sustainable, what does that really mean? And how do I as a consumer know that you're really doing it? Most companies should be doing that anyway—if for no other reason than it often flows to the bottom line. You shouldn't be wasteful. You should be thoughtful about the environment. You should be thoughtful about the resources you consume. I want to do that too. But if you say you're doing it and you're not actually following through with it, or it's not visible, then you've got a problem.

That level of transparency is increasingly something that companies struggle with because we've all grown up, in some sense, thinking about the four walls of an organization as being something that protects the brand from scrutiny from the outside or that protects them from a failed promise. And we don't want our employees to talk. It's dangerous. Who knows what could happen? But increasingly, they do.

My view is that building trust is not so much about technology as it is about policy and governance, but above all, it is about stated intent. It's about stating your purpose, and following through. The mechanics—handling data and being transparent about how you use it, and standing by the promises you make to your customers, your employees, and everyone else—are the antes. This commitment isn't ruled by technology. It's ruled by a concerted effort to govern the way we know we should behave, which translates into the way the company is perceived, and what it stands for—its purpose. And that's probably 80 percent of the problem.

That said, policy is one thing, but the thing that's more important is how do these things come alive? What do you do when you find yourself in the thick of something? That's a change management question. How do I run this? How do I deal with a problem when it pops up and it looks like it's going to run away? How do they align with our company purpose? Answering these questions and others like them, then using the answers to inform how we execute is key to building trust with customers, employees, and other stakeholders.

Product Origin and Sustainability

Increasingly, the overall quality of experience and relationships that you're building with customers and employees is predicated on the ethics of business. And there *are* ethics—it's not just something that is a 101-level introductory course in business school.

It's increasingly an important part of how we conduct ourselves, how brands conduct themselves, how we market, how we deal with care issues, how we innovate, and much more. This all goes to purpose.

For example, where products are sourced is not a unique question these days—it's out there all the time. So, a lot of companies are taking pains to say, "All our products are obtained from responsible and sustainable sources" or "We don't do animal testing" or "We sell only Fair Trade-certified coffee" and so on.

That's one half of the equation.

The other half is about how you turn your promises into reality. How do you innovate and where are you gathering these new ideas? Where do you source products and services made ethically, responsibly, and sustainably? Are you increasingly sourcing these things via your own customers? They're telling you what they want and how you should do it, so maybe involving them more in that process—which again goes to transparency—would be beneficial to you and to them. You get ideas that are going to hit your customers' real wants and needs, and they feel like their feedback is having an effect and an impact. That's a win-win if ever there was one.

When it comes to sustainability, I believe it's more important to not only talk about what we're doing to save the planet, but also to put serious thought into how we can best manage our inventory, supply chain, and manufacturing process sustainably. As much as we are deeply passionate about the world around us, we as brands and manufacturers and companies all have to fit into it in ways that are ethical *and* profitable.

There was a time you could hang a shingle, set up a factory, and have a go at it. Years ago, there weren't many consequences of doing that in most any way you decided as long as you were able to deliver on time and for a reasonable price.

Now, there are numerous tangential consequences when you start up a business. Not just for being discovered that you're not living by sustainable principles or that you may actually be contributing more carbon into the atmosphere than you're taking out of it, but rather, it's the stuff that you would find yourself hard pressed to make a case for if you're not being passionate and proactive about it. For example, companies are increasingly being asked fundamental questions like, "Do you believe in sustainability because of global warming, or do you believe in doing it because it's the right thing to do?" The real question is far simpler: Do you care about what you do—to me, my family, my community, my country, my world? Brands must be very clear about their answers to these kinds of questions.

It's very hard for companies, particularly in certain areas, to thread that needle because some of their customers might have the reverse belief about a topic. They might think that sustainability is a myth and unnecessary. Or that climate change is 100 percent a natural phenomenon that we humans have no impact on at all. Or that, whatever the global situation, the needs of their country should come first. A lot of these stands can become politically charged very quickly. So, it's incumbent on brands to figure out where the high ground is, but also to be very clear about why they've staked out that high ground and why there's a benefit—to your company, to your employees, to your customers, to the communities in which you do business, and to the world as a whole.

One thing to keep in mind is that being ethical or responsible or sustainable isn't only about doing the right thing; they can become points of differentiation for your business. You can gain a competitive advantage by amplifying your commitment to certain things and gaining the high ground as a result of that. But you've got to put it in a context that people can truly understand and get their heads around.

It's one thing to say, "We've implemented a 21-point program to offset our carbon" when hardly anyone really knows what *carbon offset* means or why they should care. But they do understand when you tell them that you're using less packaging materials and you're going to pass on some of those cost savings to your customers in the form of lower prices. They know it's a good thing, both for them and for the environment. So, why not do it?

Personal Fulfillment and Growth

Another pillar of purpose-drive experience is personal fulfillment and growth, and there are both customer and employee aspects to consider. Sometimes brands get a bit too carried away and say, "Everything I sell and serve needs to make someone feel personally fulfilled." In reality, it's unlikely that will occur in every case. Sometimes it does, and that can be satisfying; when we support certain brands because their values mesh with our own, they have a purpose we are aligned with, or they do things to make the world a better place. Or they might simply help you beyond the thing that you're immediately interested in buying. That makes me feel good and personally fulfilled that I'm supporting businesses and brands and industries that do things that make me feel like I'm having an impact.

Let's face it—it's hard for individuals to feel like they can have an impact on the world around them all by themselves. They recycle, they try not to be wasteful, they cut back on water and electricity use. But one person is just the proverbial drop in the ocean. However, when you're part of a collective of people— other customers who support the same businesses you do, businesses that are doing good in the world—then you can see that as a group you're having a definite impact. When you can enlist your customers to join with you as a brand in your efforts, you're making the customer part of your vision and not just the recipient of it.

The importance of reputation and reputational design can't be understated—standing for things, but more important, *doing* things. An example I use in social context for modern channels is that there are a number of channel platforms for certain communities of people that reward community members based on their reputation. They do things or contribute to the site in some way, and they collect rewards. Some might refer to it as gamification, which is a word I don't like. It's more reputation.

As you're swimming in data—maybe not even knowing who's who—this requires building this reputational signal both for your customers and for you. If you can be transparent about that reputational signal, meaning you do what you say you're going to do, people know where you stand, and your customers feel like they're part of something. You can start channeling things and getting value from those interactions in ways you've never before been able to do. One such example is customers who reach out to help other customers, and who have built a reputation for doing that. They are expert and as a result they're trustworthy.

Every employee needs to be encouraged to ask questions and listen. It's extremely rewarding—not only for the end customer but also for the employee—to feel like they have some degree of control. With all these vectors, the one element that seems to be in short supply is this feeling of control. If you could do these things well, people would feel like they're more in control of their own lives and the interactions they're having with people. They trust you more, and as a result, they'll probably interact with you more and buy more.

You might have employees who really go the extra mile and help customers, and not just because they're paid to do it. They're doing it because they want to help people. The reputation element of it is transparent enough to track, and it is extremely valuable. A number of years ago, in the earlier days of social media and collaboration, a large computer manufacturing company was one of the pioneers of online forums for their small business customers and technologists. The company felt that opening up a public forum like this was safe enough—the participants were tech savvy, and they were unlikely to misbehave. They were going to help one another.

We were watching some of the interactions on this computer manufacturer's help forum. What we found was a lot of regular consumers stumbled across the help forum and they posted questions there, even though it was specifically meant for technologists. And some of the technologists responded because they were small business owners themselves, or they ran a tech department in a small business. If they could answer it, they would.

I remember watching an interaction with a woman who had a problem with an optical drive on her laptop. She posted a question to the forum. One of the technologists who hung out there typed up a simple, three-step how-to for the woman—not a Q&A nor an FAQ. This was his usual approach when someone asked a question and needed help. Five minutes later, the woman posted on the forum, "That worked. I tried calling people and reading the FAQs, and nothing was resonating. Within 30 seconds this guy fixed it."

And I looked back through the logs to see how many questions this guy had answered during the two years the forum had been in existence, because he was like *gold*. I discovered that he had posted in the neighborhood of 100,000 responses during those two years. And he didn't get rewarded in any dollars-and-cents way for it. He wasn't paid money for his efforts, and he didn't even get reputational score points or anything. He just did it because that's the kind of person he was. His reward was the thanks he received when he solved someone's problem.

Being able to tease out this behavior and encourage it among employees as well as customers, people who are interested parties, is the foundation of what true community is. That's where I think, from a technology, data, and business perspective, we need to head. It's not about asking how to build better digital experiences full stop, on their own, for their own sake. It's about asking how you build communities.

It's great if you're interacting with customers and employees on Instagram and Twitter and Facebook and other social channels—you should. But more important, do you have a real community? Do you have people who are invested in the brand, in what you sell and what you provide? And are you learning from them? Are they getting more than the simple transaction value of being a customer? Are they personally fulfilled and are they growing?

Fun and Entertainment

Increasingly, we think some of the most mundane things are just that—*mundane*. In terms of the commerce experience, we focus on getting a person from A to B as quickly as possible. However, the humanistic part of me says, "Yes, you want to understand when someone's in a hurry not to get in the way of what they need." But sometimes, your customers might get some real fun and joy receiving things from you that are a welcome surprise. When you do this, you're demonstrating that you're thinking about them and you're trying to engage with them on a level that's more human than just transactional.

We're starting to see this in some brands that are offering unexpected little things to their customers. The company might send customers a fun email message based on something the customers said they were interested in on the company site. Or the company might serve customers an instant discount code when they go to check out, so they don't have to go hunt for one. The code appears with a note that says, "We noticed you've been here a lot and we thank you for your loyalty. Here's a discount code you can use right now." I call that a "digital kiss on the cheek."

All too often we tease people with offers they either don't value or can't enjoy at the moment. How often have you tried to use airline or hotel reward points only to find out there is a blackout? Or see a coupon code field just before you are about to buy something but can't find a code that works? Or worse, you may have been lured to make a purchase with an ambiguous reference to a major sale, only to find out it's for only certain items, none of which you wanted to buy? It's far better not to offer these things if you plan to make it hard for people to use them. It's not lost on the customer. It's a moment that matters and it will undermine trust if you fail to meet the expectation.

What are the digital kisses on the cheek that we can create right now—today, this very moment—that not only get people over the hump of conducting a transaction or becoming a customer, but that also surprise them and put smiles on their faces when they least expect it?

I love the example of KLM Royal Dutch Airlines. KLM was one of the first carriers to use social media to directly engage with customers when they were having problems. They first made the decision to communicate with customers via their social media channels because of the acute operational problems created by the 2010 eruption of the Eyjafjallajokull volcano in Iceland, which sent a huge plume of volcanic ash high into the sky. The ash wreaked havoc on jet aircraft engines and interrupted air travel between North America and Europe for more than a month—grounding more than 100,000 flights and affecting approximately 10 million passengers.[9]

According to Gert-Wim ter Haar, former social media hub manager for KLM, the move to social was made out of necessity—to provide customers with the highest possible levels of service. Said ter Haar in a blog post:

Not long after the eruption, every airline desk at every airport was flooded with passengers. Customers tried to get in touch with us by phone and email. Call centres couldn't handle the workload and people were put on hold for hours, so they began looking for alternatives and turned to social media.

In 2009, we had only just started exploring this new world. We had a Facebook page, a Twitter account and, like most companies taking their first steps in social media, we had no idea what we were doing. We tried posting some pictures of planes, launched a campaign, but mostly we were like kids playing in the sandbox for the first time.

Meanwhile, thousands of our customers were desperately waiting for a response. Within an hour, we had created a social media room where KLM volunteers took turns answering questions. Some would arrive at 4am wearing their business suits, so that they could do their shift and head straight through to an 8am meeting. Managers became service agents and some experienced direct customer contact for the very first time. Peter Hartman, our CEO at the time, even dropped by to see what "those crazy social people" were doing. And he loved what he saw.[10]

KLM's customers reacted well to having their questions about flights, connections, baggage, and other issues addressed quickly and by a real person—not a bot. Getting an answer is so important to people, and I just don't understand why we don't give them more answers—especially when we have the power to do it (and we almost always do).

Once the volcano calmed down, KLM asked, "How can we parlay social into a way for us to demonstrate that we're thinking about our customers instead of just responding to the problems they're having?" Thus was born the KLM Surprise Initiative.

The idea was simple: during the month of November 2010, a dedicated KLM Surprise team looked for KLM passengers at Amsterdam's Schiphol airport who had checked into Foursquare or Twitter to mention that they were waiting for their flight. When a suitable passenger was identified, the team quickly scanned their social media accounts to get a feel for them as people—more specifically, their possible likes and dislikes. A KLM flight attendant was then tasked with delivering a small, personalized gift to the surprised passenger[11]—a relax package for a runner, a New York City Lonely Planet travel guide for a passenger flying to the city, a bouquet of flowers for a passenger arriving back home from Helsinki, and so on. A photo of the encounter was taken by the team and posted to KLM's Facebook page.[12]

Although only 40 KLM passengers received gifts during the campaign's three-week duration, it generated more than 1 million impressions on Twitter as a result of tweets and retweets related to the event.

But above and beyond the numbers of tweets and retweets, what KLM did was fun for both the customers and employees. How satisfying is it for employees to see actual joy and appreciation in the faces of their customers versus frustration or disappointment? And I don't think we do enough of that. As KLM demonstrated, a gift for your customers doesn't have to be expensive, and you don't need the most technologically advanced platform in place to accomplish it. And it certainly doesn't mean you have to hoover up all the data that's available out there and monitor everything 24/7. You don't.

KLM decided they wanted to find a novel way to surprise and delight their customers. Not every single customer—there were just 40—and not with grand gestures, but what's the right level of engagement with a customer to actually humanize the process of flying? Because let's face it, we feel very dehumanized when we fly these days. There isn't a day that goes by when there isn't some horrific story about a customer losing their cool or a flight attendant dealing with some serious people problem during the course of a flight.

KLM demonstrated one thing and one thing best, which was you don't have to go that far to do something a little nice to have a big impact that people will remember and talk about. And you can't buy that kind of word-of-mouth marketing, you just can't do it. It's something that people will remember and keep talking about for a very long time. As the narrator of a KLM video documenting the Surprise Initiative explained:

> In the age of social media, doing something that creates a real smile on somebody's face is much cooler than attaching a smiley face. But most importantly, it seemed that indeed an airline could use social media to

both surprise and make a small difference to a passenger's day. And we're not just guessing, we know, because they told us, and their friends, massively.[13]

You don't have to do it for everyone, and you don't have to do it every day. It's more fun for your customers when it's unexpected, a surprise. It can quite literally make their day, especially when they were having a bad one and they weren't expecting anything. Sometimes I go to sites and they have a kind of digital Wheel of Fortune—spin the wheel and you get whatever (I assume, not exactly random) discount or tchotchke that pops up. That's not what I'm talking about, forget that.

Instead, know who I am when I visit your site, and every once in a while, just say something like, "We know that you visit our site quite a bit, but you haven't bought anything from us for a while. We did notice that you were recently looking at dining room sets, so we're going to do something special for you today. Use this code or click here for a special discount just for you." Keep Jeriad Zoghby's 4Rs in mind as you reach out to your customers: recognize, remember, recommendations, and relevance. Hit all four of these, and you'll create real moments that matter to your customers.

What are the digital kisses on the cheek that you can give to your customers, and how can you build those into an overall experience that is humanizing and amplifies your company's purpose? In the case of the KLM Surprise Initiative, the company rewarded people for flying the airline *and* it amplified its purpose of spreading happiness.

Remember how you felt as a kid when you went into a candy shop and the owner gave you an extra piece of candy just because you were a regular customer? Or you went to the donut shop, and they gave you a baker's dozen—an extra donut and not just a dozen? We were pleasantly surprised when it happened, and that's the random act of kindness from a business that we remember long after the transaction takes place.

Have some fun with your customers. Entertain them. Do it consistently and do it often enough, and you can turn your social channels into something much more powerful than just a place to sell your products and services.

Simplicity and Convenience

Sometimes we're too clever by half when we overengineer experiences, recommendations, or interactions. For example, you go to a website and it recommends things you should buy, but the site gets the recommendations terribly wrong because it doesn't have the context of your visit. Or you go to buy something and then someone tries to sell you all sorts of other things that aren't relevant to the thing that was important to you in the first place.

People talk about increasingly automating a lot of these interactions using chatbots, automated assistance, and similar technology. Where they tend to go wrong, however, is when they try to do too much with this technology, as powerful as it is, and it doesn't know its own limits.

When we talk about humanizing technology, part of it is the technology itself that is going to have to be more and more human in terms of the way it thinks and operates and so on. The only way you accomplish this is by treating technology, in many ways, like a human. Which means that there's a progressive educational process that takes time.

I have a seven-year-old child who is learning how to read. When she started out, we didn't give her a copy of *War and Peace* on day one. We're having her read things that she finds entertaining and fun and things she can remember. Truth be told, she sometimes looks at the pictures more than she reads the words, but that's okay. We don't try to get her to do too much, even though there's always pressure to enroll your kids in advanced reading classes and get them their own book deal by the time they're 12. My point is that technology is the same and we have to realize that.

A few months ago, I told a client that it's one thing to get a chatbot and stand it up, but it's quite another thing to design the right algorithms/AI going around it and getting the conversational elements right. There's a tremendous difference between informational and conversational AI. Where most organizations go wrong is when they don't understand the depth they need to go to to use technology to essentially mimic a human. "Oh well," they'll say. "Wind it up and send it on its way. We'll put it out there and get the tech team to look at the logs every so often to see where it's been able to help and where it hasn't."

My view is that we should stop placing all the responsibility on the tech team or the organization's CIO to find the right technology, stand it up, and then operate it. Rather, we should think of these new AI initiatives as educational environments— technology nursery schools where the entire community needs to help with the training, care, and feeding.

Just as there are schools for kids, there should be schools for technology. Maybe everybody in the organization wants to build a chatbot. Well, the chatbots have to be in preschool for a while and they're never let loose until they've had time to learn and engage to get the kinks out and get to the next level. There are plenty of examples of chatbots that have engaged in inappropriate conversations with users, making homophobic comments, supporting child abuse and suicide, and engaging in hate speech.[14]

Similarly, for technology, we think in terms of sprints and releases, being agile, building minimum viable products, and quickly getting something up and running. And that's all good. But a lot of this I think is where we go wrong and where technology fails so miserably. It isn't because some hapless technologist forgot a string of code, or we didn't upload the entire packet correctly and the result is that it's not pointing to the right database.

Sure, all that happens. But more important is that we don't think about our customer-facing digital systems as living things that could potentially have a soul. Ultimately, that's where we're going in terms of the Turing Test, where, in the not-too-distant future, AI will enable machines to respond in a way that makes them indistinguishable from humans. Even before we get there, we must give technology an environment to learn and grow and for us to learn and grow and think about them as well. This, I believe, is going to be the next frontier.

We forget about the importance of simplicity along the way. And when we set up our technologies to do things that they can't do because they're not at that level, we're setting up the technology—and ourselves—for failure. The systems we're building today are not as complex as we think they are, but they're not as savvy and as able to compensate for the things we never thought of or the things we thought of but we overengineered.

7

Bringing Technology and People Together in a More Human-Centric Way

I like to think of ideas as potential energy.
They're really wonderful, but nothing will happen until we risk putting
them into action.

—Mae Jemison

I hope by now you realize that the ideas I talk about in this book aren't just pie in the sky—they are actionable, attainable. Unfortunately, it's putting ideas like these into action where the majority of organizations consistently get stuck. We extol the virtues of building a better experience. We tell everyone to be transparent. We explain to organizations that they don't own their brand—that today, their brand is what customers tell them it is. We focus on all the tactical practicalities of upgrading the digital experience. But what we don't do is map out the strategic things that need to be done to make change stick.

An effective organizational strategy for humanizing digital begins with a top-down, bottom-up acceptance that we're going to do business differently. In addition, you need to have a road-map for where you're going to go and how you'll get there.

I have found that a particularly effective roadmap for humanizing digital in an organization has five steps:

1. Define the problem—walk a mile in you customer's shoes.
2. Understand the value of the moments that matter.
3. Prioritize and create the business plan for needed change.
4. Understand the implications and empower the organization to make changes.
5. Orchestrate, measure, and refine iteratively.

The cycle generally goes like this: understand the problem or opportunity, define the North Star, build the roadmap, prioritize the value of those things that you're doing, and then figure out what changes are needed to the data technologies people process and the organization. And so, very soon after having a conversation—which gets people excited about building a better experience that will in turn drive more value for the organization—people want to know what *they* need to do. They then need help managing that process. What does that look like?

It's one thing to say, "If we need to humanize everything," it's another thing to actually make it happen. This chapter provides you with a roadmap for putting the ideas in this book into practice.

Define the Problem

When was the last time you really mystery shopped your customer experience end to end? I think, given all the initiatives a major brand has going at any one time, there is a high potential to build a Franken-experience: a mishmash of unstructured (or poorly structured) channels, content, functionality, virtual, and face-to-face moments that matter. Even the best, well-intentioned brands—which invest sizable amounts of budget in data and technologies, ostensibly to make the customer experience better—often fail miserably to create experiences that are cohesive, let alone relevant or contextual.

In fact, I have often been struck by a realization that for all the clients who spend millions, sometimes billions of dollars on customer experience improvements, as a customer of the same, how little seems to have changed.

This has in fact bothered me so much that I have taken to starting every project by personally shopping the brand, seeing what it actually feels like to walk in the shoes of a customer, B2C or B2B. The results are invariably telling. When I get to the end—going channel by channel, app by app, from discovery to after-sales support—I have a really clear picture of what the problems are. I usually end up with not only a list of the tactical things that aren't right—SEO/SEM, page loads, broken links, confusing content, disjointed communications and calls to action—but I also will find one epiphany that may totally change the game.

One of the clients I reviewed sells power generators, but they were having difficulty growing their consumer business. There were many tactical things we identified they could improve, but one thing stood out above all else. We came to the conclusion after many fits and starts, and a circuitous purchase journey, that one thing that customers really wanted was not to think too much about the mechanics of the purchase: items to power, kW needed, features, and installation complexity. What they were really looking for was assurance. They craved the peace of mind knowing that if they had an outage (an increasingly likely possibility for many areas of this country) they wouldn't need to worry. Their lights would stay on, their refrigerators would work, and their heating and cooling systems wouldn't be interrupted. This realization opened up an entirely new service business for the client.

The key here is to constantly put yourself in the customer's shoes, something we often lose track of and find excuses not to do.

However, this sets the entire groundwork for identifying those critical moments that matter.

Create the Strategy/Plan

The experience roadmap or strategy/plan hopefully answers the questions: What is this experience we're trying to create? What does that feel like? Answering these questions requires identifying the opportunity, the issues, and the moments that matter. And you can't humanize digital if you don't know what moments matter to your customers. Any experience they have with your organization, whether it's face-to-face, virtual, mobile, social, or whatever it might be can have an impact. What is the experience? What is the context in which people are engaging with you?

Answering these questions is no small feat—it's a very difficult but very practical thing to do. I liken it to producing a movie. No, I've never produced a movie, but I've probably seen enough movies about producing movies that I generally know how it works. You write a screenplay, but then you've got to sell it. This provides you with the funds you need to actually create your movie. And once you've sold your film, you've got to figure out how you're going to make it come to life.

Whether you're an animator or a movie producer or writer, you're probably going to break things into a story—often in the form of a storyboard that visually lays out the story's key elements. Here's the story. Here are the elements of that story. Here's what each one of those elements looks like. Here's the tension within the scenes. A storyboard helps the director shoot the film.

I think it's exactly the same thing when we think about what kind of experience we want to create for our customers. We don't sit down and think about it in terms of producing a movie, but in truth, that's exactly what we're doing.

Traditionally, we look at the customer through a rearview mirror—a snapshot of where we've been, not where we're going.

But when you think of telling the story in the same way that you produce a movie, you don't need to look in the rearview mirror. You don't only get a snapshot of where you've been. You're seeing a movie through your windshield—in full technicolor, as it plays out in real time. That's the role of the storyboard. You can see what's coming down the pike—the context, the motivation, and much more. Says Peter Smith:

> *Forward-thinking CMOs don't separate the notion of customer experience and brand. Those two things are inexorably intertwined. Over the last two years, we saw this trend accelerate. The big observation here is that customer expectations are changing fast, and companies are not adapting to rise to the challenge. You see that in the form of traditional investments in CX not producing the returns they used to. What constitutes good CX and good experiences today are not just about creating a frictionless checkout experience.*
>
> *I think there's a lot of interesting research on Gen Z and what they expect from the brands they interact with—it's not what you traditionally expect. It's not just about having an easy checkout experience. It's not just about having good service. It's about much, much bigger things than that. I think there's a really interesting convergence in what we traditionally think of as marketing. The digital funnel from 15 years ago has been turned on its side and is now referred to as a journey. But it's still the digital funnel for all intents and purposes. That world is beginning to intersect very heavily with what I would call the experience domain.*

In the past, when you wanted to know something about your customer, you did a customer research study. And you did a segmentation. And you did quantitative and qualitative research, comprised of surveys that were hopefully from a statistically accurate sample of your target customers or prospects. You would combine that with some data indicating what these customers had actually done with you in the past, and where they got hung up in the organization and in the buying process. And then you might even sit down with some customers and do some intercepts. If you're a grocer, for example, you might talk to them while they're shopping or get them to mystery shop with you.

Or you could sit down in a darkened room and interview a focus group of customers.

That was all well and good, but to use my analogy again, they were all just snapshots in time, looking through the rear-view mirror. Why? Because by the time the research was completed, analyzed, compiled, and made available to decision makers—which could typically take anywhere from 8 to 16 weeks—your customers had already moved on, their tastes and needs shifting to new directions.

You had this wonderful, neat, three-segment strategy outlining the things that these people would most likely be receptive to, and then you had to put your plan into motion. And if you were the market researcher, you'd hand it over, and then your marketers would take one part, your fulfillment and product people would take another, and salespeople would take another. And the organization would take another six or eight weeks or more to build a program around these people, so now you're talking months before you actually do anything.

In truth, that just doesn't work any longer, if it ever did. Yes, it still takes time and effort to do this right—to do the research and build a good North Star experience. But we can accelerate the process by coming in with some perspective, not starting out empty handed. Take what you know from having been a customer, or having talked to some of your top customers, and then build that into a prototype right away.

For example, what does that storyboard look like? Let's run you through it. Does that story make sense? Then it's more iterative, it's more entrepreneurial in that you're building something right away—putting together a story that seems very plausible right now. It includes all the different pieces of that hitherto would have been separate work streams. The key to this is getting people from those work streams involved early on.

This is where the change management piece comes in, which we'll discuss in the last section of this chapter. It's a different way of working. This is getting your salespeople, marketers, customer care folks, fulfillment folks, and others joined at the hip from the beginning—right there. They're forming what is almost a new business and running it in a new way. I see people build these kinds of teams, but they don't achieve their goals because they're still not flexible or empowered enough to really make a difference.

So when I talk about creating a strategy/plan, what does that look like? Is it a 50-page document? A short paragraph? Something else?

I'm definitely *not* talking about a 50-page plan, I'm talking about getting right to what the story is—concise and direct— then beneath that story everyone agrees on, we pick out the moments that matter. We then prioritize those points because we're probably not going to do the whole thing on day one. So this comes back to being agile—being able to bite off pieces, but keeping it coherent across the entire story.

What comes out of this is a storyboard, the moments that matter, agreement on what those are in real time, a decision on what we're going to go after and how we're going to do it. That forces the conversation about exactly who we need to make this happen and how we get them to be part of this. Here's an example of how we worked with one of our clients to put a strategy/ plan together.

The organization had a centralized marketing function along with product development and fulfillment, and there was a dealer network that circled around it. But these related parts of the organization were not always aligned in terms of the experience they were trying to provide to the customer. To figure out why this was the case, we told the client that we didn't need to make a big thing of this—we wanted to cherry-pick a few people internally who had a heavy stake in this game and test the waters with them about what we were thinking in real time. We also wanted to talk with some of the dealers and some of the biggest customers to see if those things aligned.

We then told the client that we were going to come back to them, not with a 12-week study, but with an actual story, and it would be around that. We would create the personas and tell that story end to end. The story would demonstrate what we heard in terms of what we think and the moments that matter in that story. And in that story, we would show where we think those moments that matter will unfold, what channels to find the customers on. If the client was trying to find someone, where would they find them and how would they find them if they weren't already their customer? Would they walk in the door, or would the client have to do some research? Would they have to do outreach, and if so, how would they do that? We would show them an example of that.

For example, a particular customer might be a fleet owner, and they wouldn't be interested in the main product itself, but in the parts for it. What does it feel like to be a parts manager with that customer and would they want to be able to see those parts and where they fit and how they might be installed? We've applied some basic assumptions and principles to it that people now have shifted. Whatever experience they're having—whether it's B2B, B2C, or whatever it is—they're converging in terms of what people expect in terms of the experience.

Traditionally, a customer would pick up the phone and call your sales department to get an order started, then they'd fax over an order form, and you'd approve it and fax it back, or maybe do the back and forth by email. If the customer already had an account set up, great, but if they didn't, they would have to go through a whole process to do that.

What I'm saying is forget all that. Everyone expects to be able to go into a cart and order and know what that experience is going to feel like, because that's what we're all used to. So how would *we* do that? We would put together a physical map with visuals to graphically show what every step of that storyline is going to be, what the moments that matter are going to be for people, meaning what are the sticking points, where they could say, "No, it's too much trouble," or "I didn't find what I needed and I'm going to go someplace else."

We took this journey map and in the workshop, we worked with all the people who would be key stakeholders across all the business functions we thought those moments that matter would touch. We did a real-life exercise saying, let's assume the experiences we architected were solid, which most people said they were, but then we would determine how best to enable them. We already had in mind that you could use the technologies and platforms we already know you have. But you're not using them in concert today, so here's what that would take. And we just went through everything that was a specific channel being used at the time, the conversation or interaction that a customer might have, the motivations that each of the characters had.

We're back to my movie analogy again, which is that the motivation of the mothership is going to be very different from the motivation of the dealership versus the motivation of the customer. So, how do you rationalize those?

We didn't put together a pretty deck; we literally put together a poster scroll, everything that someone was going to go through, and then all the pressure points, those moments that matter. But we also got people to figure out and prioritize the things we thought had the greatest value by putting a price tag on them. We said, "If you do these three things, this will lift your boat by $500 million. If you do these 10 things, it might only lift the boat $650 million. So, let's figure out the three or four things to do first that will give you the greatest return. It's not that we think you shouldn't do the others, but let's start with these because they will enable everything else to happen."

We apply that movie producer's approach to everything we do now. In many ways, that's the way we do design thinking. We try to figure out the context, and then literally get that on paper so people can see it and react to it. Sometimes we go straight to prototype and just show our clients what that would look like.

Sure, you can spend months doing all the research, but where it really gets interesting—and where people really get it—is when you show them what that would look like and feel like. There are lots of different ways to do that, including with a simple PowerPoint presentation, which I recently did with a client. I wanted to articulate what this thing could be based on actually having been a customer. This provider wants to become a big player in a particular product niche, and if you look at that arena today, much of it is very product centric. Everyone says, "Here's my product and this is what it does. I'll ask you a few questions, set up an appointment, and we'll send a salesperson over to tell you what you really need."

But having put myself in those shoes and walked a mile or two, that's not what I felt I wanted. I wanted someone to answer the first question, which is, "Do I need this particular product?" And be honest. There should be some good reasons for me to consider purchasing this fairly expensive product for my home, and there might be equally good reasons why I should not. As I spoke with the client, I saw all the heads nodding, but I couldn't tell if they really understood what my ideal experience would look like.

So, I took PowerPoint and turned it into an animation tool to create a storyboard. I said, "I'm going to make the cursor go up here to this. I'm going to go to Google and do a search, and I'm going to show you where I ended up. I'm also going to show you where I wanted to end up, but I didn't. And I'm going to take your website and I'm going to just cut and paste it really quick to show you what it could be."

The epiphany that came out of it was don't *not* answer the question your customer asks, then pawn them off on another person they didn't even reach out to in the first place. The more people you put in the way, and the more obstacles you create, the more likely they'll go somewhere else, and you'll lose the sale.

When you look at your strategy, you might think, "This is a great story—it's going to be a fantastic experience." And you're probably right about that, but putting your strategy into motion is crazy hard—especially the larger the organization you lead.

Turning your organization on a dime to be as responsive as you want it to be is extremely difficult, but it can be done.

Very quickly you must figure out what your constraints are. The instant killer for any new initiative is when someone says, "Yeah—that sounds great, but I can't do it." It's always the "yeah, but" that gets you because so often the easiest and the least risky thing to do in life is to do nothing. We're always fighting inertia. To overcome inertia, ask, "Freeing ourselves of reality, how would we do this? Are there some practical things that we could put in place in the way of technologies and data?"

Contextualize the Data

The first question I usually ask, since this all hinges on data to a certain degree to make happen, is this: What data do we have and what data do we not have? So, we map that very quickly.

Most every company today has data on customer purchases, but they're often not even using a fraction of the data they've got. The other thing is that there's all this new data swirling around all day, every day, that very few people have access to at all, because they're not even looking at it, or they're not sharing it in the organization. And more important, they're not synthesizing it into a "so what?" So, people are put off because they think it's all too abstract.

Online home interior design companies like Decorist, Havenly, or Modsy (which I mentioned in the Introduction) are start-ups with a business model that is quite impressive. And I don't say that just because I had a good experience with these services, which I did. What was really interesting to me was that at the very beginning of the customer engagement process, these services got me to take a psychographic test, even though they don't call it that. They asked questions like, "What colors do you like? Here's a range for you to select from," and "What styles do you like? Here are some examples of what we mean." This is all presented visually on their website.

So, I might respond that I liked a style that is somewhere in between minimalist and midcentury modern. Then they show you a bunch of photos of those kinds of designs, and they also invite you to point them to more photos online that reflect your style—you can give them URLs from Pinterest or photos from Instagram or most any other image source. They need to know what the room currently looks like, so you provide them with a number of photos of the space—you can use your smartphone to take the photos and upload them, nothing fancy. You provide them with the room's rough dimensions—height, length, width—and let them know where the doorways and windows are. That's the start of your collaborative process with this company.

What's particularly intriguing to me about the process is that the data they get from their customers probably exists nowhere else in the world—they have a unique perspective into a person's living space and their preferences, a real window into their soul. How? They get that information because their customers have willingly shared that data with them. And they do so because the company is going to provide them with a really nice, 3D room design in return—they can even buy the furniture and décor they see in their design directly from them as a form of digital concierge. And if these services are successful in designing one room for a customer, they'll likely end up doing all their rooms.

I personally believe that *every* industry could start thinking of a similar proxy. But when it comes to data, we tend to think very flat—very one-dimensional. This customer bought that item on Tuesday, and it was worth this much. This other customer bought that other item yesterday, and it was worth this much.

That doesn't tell us the whole story. It's the context of *why* they bought it—that's what is most interesting to us. A lot of the things that we try to do in the practical terms to get to the next level is figure out the textual data, the intersections of data. And wherever there are gaps, we try to figure out how to fill in those gaps. And some of it is the real-time data—not real-time purchase data, which is easy to get. The real-time data we're looking for include how many hundreds of millions of people are out there every day talking about something? Something that bothers them, irritates them, frustrates them, or makes them happy or joyful, or that makes them want to share something because it's inspirational.

There are billions upon billions of conversations, totally unstructured and in the public domain, which most organizations use only a fraction of. Or organizations allow the preconceived notions they have about their customers to determine what conversations they listen to. Says Sprinklr chief revenue officer Luca Lazzaron:

> *I have companies that listen to their customers and they do it thinking first about them versus their assumptions. But the majority of companies act like they did 20 or 25 years ago—they decide the strategy, they decide that the market or the consumer needs that product or that payoff or that special initiative or whatever. And then they go and use their technology to validate their assumptions. That doesn't work because then they only listen to what they want to hear. That's the problem.*
>
> *Today's best companies flipped the script. They had to go out there without any assumptions and understand what their customers are thinking about their brand and their products or services. Technology plays a big role in this if you use it properly because you can know real time, or very close to it, what every single customer is thinking about you—they're saying it. So, you only have to go and capture those conversations without the bias of only looking for the things that you care about because you have made your own assumptions.*

So how do you identify the conversations you should be listening to or reading about or gathering in whatever way you find most effective? This is where we start getting into the technology side of things.

There are plenty of technologies available these days that allow you to listen to your customers—to be a fly on the wall—which is the most important thing you can do. You can listen directly from your own modern channel accounts, whether it's Facebook or Twitter or whatever they might be, but in truth, not everyone's even responding to direct messages. A customer sends a company a direct message via social and says, "I have a problem," and they get nothing in return but crickets. That's the first level, the low-hanging fruit that every organization should be targeting.

The next level up gives you a sense of the broad themes of what customers you're interested in talk about, think about, get worried about, and so on. And there are plenty of technologies that you can use to do that, including Sprinklr, Brandwatch, Hootsuite, Social Studio by Salesforce, and many others. There's just a whole panoply of different technologies that help provide a framework for doing this kind of work.

But it's how you use them, not necessarily just what you have, that makes the difference. And, going through this sort of exercise forces a conversation, and hopefully it helps provide a roadmap for utilization of those platforms and technologies.

Rework the Organization

Reworking the organization is a big deal in most companies and you might ask who should drive this effort. That's a good question, and I'll answer it in a few different ways. Traditionally, there was always separation of church and state, and it's still true. You go into most any company and there's a marketing organization, a sales organization, a service organization, and if your company is large enough, you've also got a chief information officer (CIO) and a chief technology officer (CTO). And when it came to things like making technology choices, it was often the CIO who was tasked with that responsibility—there was a separation of church and state. And when it came to marketing and campaigns, there was also a separation of church and state, and the same for business operations. The silos were built very intentionally, and they were strong and sturdy.

Some organizations had a kind of functional hybrid where some of these elements—for example, operations—would see themselves as internal consultants. And depending on how the business was set up, whether you had an internal transfer mechanism for moving budget about, for getting things that you need, that was one thing organizations put in place to get a handle on all this stuff.

So, a lot of the operational organizations within an enterprise would say, "We're going to treat all our business owners and stakeholders as customers, and we're going to offer them different things." That was good and a step in the right direction, but it didn't necessarily break down any of the silos or other barriers because we still had that strict separation of church and state in effect between technology and campaigns and content and research and so on.

The good news is that some organizations have started to bring these groups together in some fashion. They recognize that it may not be good enough to expect their technology group to make a decision on their own, even if they're seeing themselves as an internal vendor and trying to be responsive. It's more than being responsive. It's more about being a thought partner and having a real stake in the business. You can create real ownership by awarding part equity to these different groups based on what they achieve working together within the organization.

Where I think it gets really interesting is when you start giving people joint responsibilities—for example, *in theory* everyone should be a marketer. If you talk to a customer, if you provide an experience to them, then you should have some marketing knowledge. By the same token, analytics has typically existed in a vacuum, and that's where the heavy lifting happens. But in truth, every group really needs to be somewhat analytic.

If you're going to be a data-driven organization, if you're going to use data to help you make decisions and make things happen in real time—not letting it dominate you—then you have to have pretty good sense of data, whether you're a marketer or a salesperson or anyone else. So you'd have to figure out what's important and what isn't very quickly, and then build that into the systems that you're using to enable these experiences to occur.

I see the CMO of the future as one part CIO, one part sales lead, one part customer care lead, and always thinking about that experience because otherwise the experience falls apart. It's not an experience, it's just a collection of experiences, and that's what you often find with organizations today. The marketing experience is typified by how many emails you get a day or the latest offer you get when you go online and there's a pop-up interstitial.

If you think about technology, it's no longer just the nuts and bolts of picking a platform and then enabling it so that people have access to it and can use it. Again, it's about being in the business sufficiently to know that it's important once you've made those investments and you've gotten a consensus around it, and everybody uses it and is getting value out of it.

That means that your job is not done once you've made the selection and stood it up and done everything that you feel you needed to. It now pushes technology into the sales organization, into the marketing organization, into the analytics organization, and everywhere else it needs to go. These roles are all going to have to be redefined, which is where change management comes in.

Manage Change

Everyone talks a big story about change management, but when push comes to shove, there's often not enough time to put a focus on it—everyone is trying to get everything done faster than ever and keep the organization moving forward. And if they do decide to put some of their focus on change management, they'll say, "We just need to get people trained up and conversant." But that's not going to work—you need to get people to work completely differently and just doing training isn't going to cut it.

For organizational change to stick, you need to have the right skill sets in the right places; people do need to be trained, but deeply enough that they have the ability to make a difference; and they have to be able to think, not just do what you've outlined. If everyone is invested in the business, then they will be invested in the experience, and the experience will constantly get better and better. Employees are thinking like merchants, or they're thinking like people who own the business, and that I think is the ingredient most often missing—that sort of heart and soul of the business. All the things that we're talking about in this chapter are the things that ladder up to enable that.

I recently worked on a project with a client using this kind of approach. We came in with a strong point of view and a proof of concept. We weren't waiting for them to send us a request for proposals, and we weren't waiting for the customer to come to us and say, "This is broken, come fix it." We started this whole conversation with some of the folks who know key clients and what they're struggling with in quick serve, particularly franchise quick serve.

One of the perennial issues when you're running your business—and it's getting worse in many ways if you're a franchisee—is it that it's ultra-hard to do all the other things you need to do, like marketing and looking at data and analyzing the data to come up with new programs, while also balancing that against central corporate marketing. Because the corporate parents don't encourage or allow much in the way of off-the-cuff, extemporaneous campaigns, it's not always easy for a franchisee to build real community and to make a real difference locally.

In the case of a quick-serve, fast-food restaurant, there are probably three down the road and two over on the other side of the street that are all within 5 or 10 minutes of one another.

While your core customers may usually be dedicated to you, depending on their immediate situation—they may be in a big hurry to get their fast-food fix, or they may have a taste for fried chicken instead of a burger at the moment—in other words, they might not think of your restaurant on every occasion. They might think of someone else, just because it's closer or less busy or they serve the spicy chicken sandwich they're craving at that moment. We're currently in that mode where it's hard to just differentiate on the basis of the food experience itself.

When you start to think about how you might keep customers coming back again and again, which is the name of the game, there's always more you can do to market to them. But more important, there's *lots* more you can do to develop and engage with your local community. It's the people who live in the area who are going to be your loyal, top customers forever. We looked at all kinds of things that we could be doing, and the thing that struck me as an epiphany goes back almost 10 years ago. It was a time when social media was still fresh and we were trying to figure it out and, of course, we still are in many ways.

I was asked to speak at a conference in Paris, and despite my quick response to the invitation (Yes!), I was also painfully aware of how little I felt I could bring to the conversation at the time. But I was heartened by another guy invited to speak who also came from Chicago. He was the social media leader for a large, national fast-food chain—a brand that had suffered some hits.

The thrust of the conversation for our conference session was that social media can be a double-edged sword. You can use it to reach more people, create greater engagement with them than ever before, and build trust and transparency. But if you're not careful, you can also destroy trust quite literally overnight. If something bad happens in one of your restaurants or stores, and someone videotapes it and posts it on Twitter or Facebook, that can do immeasurable damage to your brand, quite literally in hours or even minutes. And it's hard to get your credibility back once it's been destroyed in that way.

The other guy from Chicago was extremely entrepreneurial. Although he had a very limited budget to work with, he started experimenting with social media to see if it could make a positive impact on his brand. He knew exactly who his target customer was—young people—and he knew the behaviors he wanted to drive—namely, more frequent visits to the restaurants and larger orders placed. His question was: "Where do these customers hang out, and how can I get to them?"

He figured out that these young people weren't sitting at home reading newspapers and watching TV like their parents were, so advertising there wouldn't pay off. Instead, they were all on social media and they were talking with one another about the things that were important to them. So, with this knowledge, he put together a very crafty guerrilla marketing campaign based on social media.

The first thing that was really great about what he was doing was that he was just intuitively amazing in terms of engaging with people and using these social media tools in a very effective way with photos and video and memes so on. Second, he was just genuine—he really cared. No matter what he posted, it wasn't just a throwaway, it wasn't just the content of the day. He gave his customers real value and a great experience in exchange for their time.

He told us a story about one of his campaigns that was focused on his community. It's no secret that Chicago's weather is often terrible. A few years ago, we had a really bad snowstorm, and the city was paralyzed; you couldn't go out, you couldn't do anything. So, this manager decided he was going deliver pizzas to people in spite of the weather. If his customers shared a photo with him delivering the pizza, he'd give them a credit for a free one next time. He was the ShamWow guy of pizza—very engaging, very genuine, very intuitive—and the campaign worked.

He built his own marketing empire, and he demonstrated that you could do it completely vertically. You could create the product, you could market it, and you could sell it. And it was important to him that it wasn't just a one-man show—he got other people who worked for him to do these same sorts of things and it paid off, turning around the company's fortunes.

That stuck with me because here was something that you would just not pay much attention to because you think it's a commodity. But this guy showed that the fast food he was selling was much more than that—it was an experience.

And he even went further. This was in 2008—the beginning of the Great Recession—and people were struggling to get jobs. So, he invited customers to post their jobs and he tweeted the postings out to people. He was getting these college kids to the point where they felt like they were part of a little minicommunity, and they would exert brand preference because they felt that they had made a real connection with a person—more than just the product. That's something we tend to overlook as marketers. The human element always trumps everything else when it comes to marketing.

This social media leader didn't have huge budget. He didn't have amazing technology. He used what was there. But he injected his experience and his infectious personality into everything he did. It became as much about him as it was about the product, and it worked. It demonstrated that you *can* do a lot with a little if you just do it right.

8

Realizing a New Vision for Building Community and Loyalty

Loyalty cannot be blueprinted. It cannot be produced on an assembly line. In fact, it cannot be manufactured at all, for its origin is the human heart—the center of self-respect and human dignity. It is a force which leaps into being only when conditions are exactly right for it—and it is a force very sensitive to betrayal.

—Maurice R. Franks

When we first started this little experiment in social digital, the idea was to build more transparency. How wonderful this experiment will be because it will for the very first time give customers a direct voice in real time. There's nothing more democratic than that, right? We used to spend our time—8-, 16-week studies—doing segmentation work with multivariate and conjoined analysis to try to understand who the best customers in our market were, what they wanted, and the nature of their demand.

But when social hit, there was this idea that you would have a continuous view into that, and customers would tell you what they wanted—they would be proactive. You wouldn't have to go hire a bunch of people that look like your target market and spend time in a market research center doing interviews or panel discussions. You could, for the very first time, get the word direct from the horse's mouth, sift through that, and hopefully find transparent truth in it. And not only that, but be able to interact and engage with those individuals in real time.

Trust to me was an implicit, if not explicit, promise that drove this entire experiment in the first place, which is why we're going to put on our listening caps, we're going to hear you out, we're going to respond, and we're going to be better. And you the customer are going to help us build our businesses.

In truth, some of that did occur, but we quickly degenerated into the idea that we like to listen to people, all this organic stuff is useful, but we really just want to get to the markets as quickly as possible with a story, with our message. And if people respond, great—more power to them. But we don't have enough time in the day to listen to all of our customers and respond to them. In truth, we listened for a bit and then it got too hard.

And that's the rub in terms of why there was a promise and an expectation of trust, but it feels almost like betrayal. If I'm a marketer, I think, "Oh great I can use all this data, all these conversations—millions and billions of conversations every day—to hone my message, and in real time get something out to people that's going to make them respond." It's going to make them do something. Markets may use about 1/10 of 1 percent of that information, and more often than not, just the high notes.

But it's this whole thing about making a customer *do* something that is the heart of the problem—it's what undermines trust and loyalty in the first place. As a customer, I don't want to be made to do something. I might be willing to hear you out, but I don't want to be made to do something by you. And then there's the insidious sense people have that instead of hearing them out on things they're interested in and responding and being receptive and personalizing things in a way that's meaningful to them, their data is just being used to sell anything and everything to them. I don't know anyone alive who thinks that the flood of data being collected about them are being used to benefit individuals and customers in any meaningful way.

Of course, the history of marketing has always had a focus on trying to get people do something—to buy a product. If you believe the marketers, the product will make you smell better, it'll make you smarter, it'll make you look better, it will make you more popular with potential mates. You name it. And even though organizations started to use these new channels to engage with customers, somewhere down the line we substituted influencers for catchy slogans, still with the same intent—to get people to view our message whatever it takes.

With digital, it still feels like we're trying to force a traditional straitjacket onto this channel when in truth we could use it to open up so many more opportunities for real connection to create marketing pull, rather than just the push. And we see that in terms of some of the better brands out there that engage with their customers beyond the product or the service. Brands engage with customers on other things. They build real communities.

I like Apple in many ways because the campaigns I've seen that I respond to the most are focused on the visual aspects of the company's products. They have great designers, and when you walk into their stores, the experience is unique and quite special compared with other retailers. The Apple website has a similar design aesthetic—slick and minimalist. It may be one of the main reasons I buy their products, but I think there's more they do that is intangible.

A few years ago, Apple did something that was really interesting to me. They invited customers to share things they produced with their Apple products as part of their campaigns, perhaps most notably the photos they were taking with their iPhones. In 2019, the company launched its Shot on iPhone Challenge, with a panel of judges reviewing worldwide submissions and then selecting 10 winners. The winning photos became the basis of advertising campaigns in Apple stores, online, and on billboards in major cities.[1]

I think that's probably one of the single most interesting things in terms of building community with a product company that I've ever seen. It's interesting to me because this is a way to see your customers as true human beings—not just numbers in a report. These are the creations of humans having real experiences, real *human* experiences. There's not a photo among the winners that isn't evocative of someone's travel experience or family life or city scene or other very real human experience.

I'm reminded of the TV series *Mad Men* when Don Draper took on the challenge of coming up with an ad campaign for the Kodak Carousel slide projector. Of all the episodes, that was the one that most got to me on an emotional level.

Going in, the Kodak executives wanted Don Draper's ad agency to emphasize the amazing technology built into the product—that the company had reinvented the wheel (they even suggested calling this new product the "Wheel"). Don was getting pressure from his advertising firm's head of account services to give the Kodak executives what they wanted, but instead, he stepped back and examined his own life. He pulled some slides from his family's collection of key events and put them in the projector.

Don realized that people aren't buying a projector. They aren't buying a product. They're buying a way to relive the most important memories they have from their own lives. So, instead of pitching the Kodak Wheel projector, Don aimed for the human side, tugging at customers' (and the executives') heartstrings—the visceral motivations humans have to remember the important moments of their lives. He told the Kodak executives in the pitch meeting:

Nostalgia literally means the pain from an old wound. It's a twinge in your heart far more powerful than memory alone. This device isn't a spaceship, it's a time machine. It goes backwards and forwards. It takes us to a place where we ache to go again. It's not called the "Wheel," it's called the "Carousel." It lets us travel the way a child travels. Round and around and back home again. To a place where we know we are loved.[2]

Don's pitch turned the projector into a metaphor for the circle of life. What it hit on was that human, visceral element that we keep coming back to when we talk about humanizing digital. And that's in many ways where the miss is, where people could be using their digital platforms more effectively to get into a trusting relationship with their customers. And it doesn't have to be a deep, buddy-buddy relationship. It just has to be a relationship—something that's defined by more than "I hand you my money, you hand me your products, and hopefully I don't complain about it."

It's more about buying a product that's enabled me to do something that I'm proud of or that's helped me resolve a problem I was worried about, and that started a dialogue. And now I have a chance to share that dialogue or engage with you in that dialogue as part of a community. That is where true loyalty lies.

You see this done particularly well with some of the more exotic automobile brands, where passionate customers start their own communities. There is, for example, the Porsche Club of America for avid Porsche owners in the United States (https://www.pca.org/), Tesla Owners Online for fans of Tesla automobiles (https://teslaownersonline.com/), The Maserati Club for Maserati owners (http://themaseraticlub.com/), and many more. These organizations host racing clinics, autocrosses, car shows, charity drives, and other social events, and are often supported by the manufacturers.

And the thing about it is that it's not only for those people in the community who are passionate. You might have a healthy digital community that has 10,000 people in it, whether it's a group of people who are fans of Craftsman tools, or Tesla cars, or making quilts, and the pattern is almost always the same: it's pyramid shaped. There's a small number of extremely motivated people at the top of the pyramid who organize the community and plan events and keep the conversation going. They post questions. They answer questions. And most important, they share things. And when it's working really well, they share things that other people react to in a very positive way.

That unlocks something you simply cannot buy with pure marketing dollars. It's more than programmatic—it goes straight from the head to the heart, like Don Draper's pitch for the Kodak Carousel projector. You're building trust because you're part of a group, which is a very human thing. We don't trust someone until they're a part of our group or vice versa. It's in our DNA, a trait that has evolved with us through time and that has kept us alive as a species. Don't trust anyone until you know you can trust them.

No matter what technology we've created, our genetic and behavioral heritage as humans forces us right back into that same model, because that's what's kept us alive as a species. We engage with, we enjoy the company of, we become friends with, and we build our own cohorts based on trust. That trust is hard fought and easily lost. From a geopolitical standpoint, we do that through diplomacy in politics. If you want something from your neighbor, we've found that rather than shooting missiles and sending in your troops and just going in and taking it, sometimes it's better to work with them and build trust. Both nations can survive and thrive as a result, and their citizens can be happy.

The same thing applies here. Marketers seem to think of this as a zero-sum game—if someone wins, someone's got to lose. More often than not, that someone who lost was the customer because marketers were trying so hard to get them to do something and they hadn't taken enough time to build their cohort with customers. This is a mistake because when you take the time to build genuine trust with your customers, those people are going to keep coming back and they're going to be spreading word-of-mouth, positive vibes to all the people you want to get to be customers as well. That's just a reoccurring theme.

Again, I think as marketers, as businesspeople, we often miss that. We say we understand it. We pay lip service to it, for sure.

And the best salespeople are naturally good at making friends. Whether you're selling cars or insurance or your restaurant—the best salespeople possess a kind of interpersonal magic that is uniquely powerful. Their magic is in reading people and understanding their motivations and being able to quickly build trust and rapport with them. And that hasn't necessarily carried over and translated into the digital world.

Building a Digital Trust Environment

After years of working with lots of clients *and* being on the client side, I have learned that when you deliver the product you say you're going to deliver, and you do it on time, you'll naturally build trust with your customers. Of course, that's got nothing really to do with digital other than maybe digital helps you do some of those things. Digital is table stakes in the marketing game.

But more important, now that people have so many other channels that they can go to, you can no longer believe that what works well in one channel is going to work well in all of them—that's just not the case. But what you can do is think about the commonalities, the things that never change much no matter what channel a customer is in, whether they're mobile, or on the web, or interacting with you in a store environment, or somewhere else.

Certain principles are self-evident. For example, the nature of people's demand is fairly consistent. The way people want to be treated is also fairly consistent, though the idea of the value of it has changed. Customers want to feel like they got something out of the bargain that's more than just the sum total of the parts.

To that end, when you make people feel they're alone in the transaction or in the story, that's when they're most vulnerable and probably more prone to go and do something else. They're frustrated and they feel like they have no one to turn to. And your technology can either assist with that and you can think about it holistically, or you can continue with disjointed silos and demarcation lines that create barriers for your customers—and for your employees. We need to create a seamless feel across marketing campaigns and marketing activities.

But the sales process and the technology that are used to make that brand promise come alive—whether you're in store or online or doing web, or on mobile—those are the things that you must think about end to end. If you don't, and if you fail to deliver on the brand promise in the campaigns you run, your customers will have bad experiences, you'll break the trust you've built with them, and they'll actively seek out better and more trustworthy alternatives.

This problem arises when the marketers haven't been talking to the commerce people in their organization, and the commerce people haven't really figured out what the overall brand promise piece is and how to make that better. The marketers therefore can't help them. Salespeople change the game in terms of getting people not to abandon their cart.

We've traditionally thought about these things in very compartmentalized ways. Therefore, the solutions available to us are also very compartmentalized. So, we get a piece of technology, and we say, "Oh, it can do that. That might be better than what I have." And in truth, it may or may not be better from a technology perspective, but what's important is it's not going to have any impact unless you actually think about what it's going to take to make that come alive in a meaningful way across the entire customer experience.

I belong to three or four different loyalty programs for travel brands—airlines, hotels, and rental cars—and when I'm traveling, I know what to expect from each of them. With my airline loyalty program, for example, I know what kinds of perks I will get based on the membership tier I have attained based on my mileage—seat upgrades, special check-in lines, no baggage fees, and so on. They're generally good at managing those expectations and trying to make up for them when they fail. The same is true for the hotel and rental car loyalty programs to which I belong.

No one takes a trip thinking in a compartmentalized way about the individual components of their trip—the rental car, the hotel, the airline. We look at the trip holistically, as an entire experience, although what we get from each of the brands involved is something quite different. If one of the brands fails—say, your airplane flight is canceled and the next available flight doesn't leave until the following morning—it can spoil your entire trip.

This I believe is where the new frontier is—the context of people's needs, their demand, their journeys, their stories. And this is where it gets really interesting because it's all about the human piece again because human experiences aren't colored by just one thing. Customers aren't immediately happy just because they got their rental car on time when their plane arrived four hours late. The overall experience hinges on a variety of interdependent pieces.

We should ask: Are there opportunities now to think about this experience as holistic, even if it's not my specific brand? Are there things I can do to make up for a bad experience, a one-off in another part of this customer's journey? Can we do something to build stronger bridges of trust with our customers? Says Luca Lazzaron:

> *We need champions. And to have these champions, first, we have to identify them and then we have to build trust with them. And building trust with them to me is across three different dimensions. First, on the solution that you're offering them. Second is your company, your brand— who you are—and if they want to deal with you. And third is the people with whom they interact. When you have confidence and trust across these three dimensions, you're never going to lose it.*

And I think that there is so much more that you can do through digital to build that trust, but you have to be very intentional across these three dimensions because just doing one isn't going to work.

Keep in mind that brands don't have to move heaven and earth to create great experiences for their customers and build trust. While it may sound a bit corny, it's amazing what something as simple as a smile can do for someone. You can be having the worst day ever, but if someone is able to make you smile for even just a moment, that can make the day much better and much more palatable.

Context is king. Having the wrong context or an incomplete picture of who a customer is is not where any company should be today. Brands have so much data available to them—from all sorts of different sources—that they should be able to know where their customers are in any given situation. And the trade-off customers expect from a trust standpoint is that they're giving you this information in the expectation that you will do something meaningful for them. They're not just giving it to you because they feel like giving it away, or because they don't have any privacy lens on.

Of course, many of us feel uneasy giving all this personal information away to brands, especially when there's no immediate benefit to us. In fact, I think there's a fatalism going on right now with people and their data, the idea that, "I gave my information to Google, and they do whatever they want with it—I can't even imagine."

In truth, Google doesn't do that. They are very targeted with the information they gather. But we feel as human beings as though our innermost thoughts, secrets, and ideas are exposed to the world and that someone could do something with them—and not necessarily something good. In the darkest recesses of our imagination, we may become concerned that people will do all sorts of bad things with the information they gain about us. That's an inflection point for trust.

Building trust isn't something you can leave to chance. I suggest applying the following framework to build long-term trust with your customers:

First, start thinking about customer experience holistically, from end to end. You can't think about customer experience in components. People don't behave that way and people don't think that way. None of us do. We think about the complete story that we're going through in any given moment or day.

Next, build programs, campaigns, marketing programs, and businesses around the idea that not everything is going to go right. We don't take enough time to think about all the things that could possibly go wrong and what we could do to make the experience better for someone when it does wrong, because it inevitably will.

Be aware of your customers' context, which involves understanding exactly where someone is in that journey. And it's not just journey mapping, it's figuring out what pieces of data could give you a signal in real time that says, "I'm here to buy some toothpaste," versus, "I'm here to get a pain reliever for my child who has a temperature of 104." There's a big difference. Customers want a different experience, so how do you tease out that context? It's very doable.

Put a priority on getting the experience right, standing behind your brand promise, getting the context right, and using data in an appropriate way that both protects your customers and encourages them to share things that enable you to make their lives better.

Finally, build real community. Not a loyalty program—I'm talking about *real* community. The most loyal loyalty program you're ever going to have is when you've got people who are talking with you *and* engaging with one another.

When I was working for Sears and we built our community around Craftsman tools, a quarter of a million people joined in the first year. Some of these people were hardcore—they really wanted to talk and share and ask questions and get answers to questions. They were our loyalty-on-steroids customers—engaged and proactive. Most were already immensely loyal and involved with the brand, and they didn't wait for us to provide them with opportunities.

We looked at the logs and conversations in the forums over the Thanksgiving holiday, just before Black Monday. Quite apart from us, a group of parents who wanted to prepare for the holiday season started their own sort of holiday gift circle to get ideas, suggestions, reviews of the best gifts that they could get their kids based on their age and interests. They literally held a virtual sleepover the night before Black Monday, before the stores opened. They were saying things like, "And I saw PlayStations at this store, and here's what you have to do to go get one."

For me, that was the most human thing I'd ever seen. They felt like they knew one another and so they trusted the advice and opinions of their virtual family. We weren't trying to control everything that our community was doing, we were simply facilitating their interactions. And if we could help, we would. But the best way to help in some cases was to enable them to interact, to encourage and foster and curate the conversations between them, and make the reviews and the forum posts and Q&A come alive for people and curate those so that it was easy for the next person to find.

All those things together help build a real trust-based program via digital *and* via live interactions in the twenty-first century.

Creating a Digital Bill of Rights

Trust is a uniquely human emotion. You can't always define what trust is; you just know it when you see it. It goes back to the proverbial dilemma that most brands have, between spending more on acquiring new customers and investing in retaining existing ones. They push campaign after campaign, bombarding customers with email and programs on digital. And when they're successful, they say, "Well, I know it's a formula. Out of the 1 million pieces of creative I send out, 2 to 5 percent of the recipients will sign up for this or convert for that, and I know that I've had a successful campaign. And if I've controlled the cost per thousand (CPM) on all of that, then I know it's cost effective, and I can prove that the marketing I did was worthwhile."

Harder to prove, but I think far more valuable, is this: "I built a community of really dedicated customers who are engaging with the brand in meaningful ways. And by the way, I did an analysis and they're our most valuable customers. They're telling us stuff that doesn't exist anywhere else. They're telling us what they want. They're giving us advice. Sure, some complain— that's going to happen. But they're giving advice and they're working through problem solving with each other, which is also great because sometimes being observant on the sidelines is the best thing you can do. Just shut up and listen."

You may be familiar with the acronym CPI, which usually stands for consumer price index. Gene Cornfield uses a different kind of CPI in his consulting and strategy: *customer performance indicators*. A good example of customer performance indicators in action is the GEICO tagline, "15 minutes could save you 15 percent or more on car insurance." The CPIs are time and money. And if you can build your entire experiential process around how you help customers save time in getting a quote and save money based on your underwriting performance, then you're achieving those CPI outcomes. Says Gene:

> If we can establish the outcomes that the customer cares about, and we start to measure and identify that there is a direct, predictable correlation between how we perform on a CPI—the outcome a customer values—and how we perform on a business KPI—the outcome a company values—then two things happen. One, employees are no longer

incentivized to just do whatever they've got to do to achieve the KPI, including manipulating customers. Two, employees are now incentivized to help the customer achieve the customer's intended outcome. A byproduct of this is better performance on the business outcome because that correlation or causation has been previously established.

Sure, KPIs are still important, but if employees are measured partially on CPIs, which are basically aligned with how they help customers achieve what's important to them, then how employees treat the customer changes and customers feel it. They're thinking, "Wow, you're being surprisingly helpful to what I want."

This impacts sales, this impacts loyalty, this impacts net promoter score, and this impacts all the internal-facing vanity metrics. You improve your business performance by improving how you're performing for your customers, but you need CPIs in order to do that.

That's where we need to go. But inertia—the way we've done things for the past 100 years—gets in the way, because if you control your CPMs, and you can prove that you got out to a wide audience, and they did something that you wanted them to do, no one gets in trouble for that. But if you get into the messy world of building community and trying to respond in real time to people's needs, trying to personalize things in a contextual way, trying to acknowledge and be transparent about the value exchange between personal information and commerce, that's where it gets tricky, because there is no specific digital bill of rights at this point.

Which brings us to the topic of a digital bill of rights, which we introduced in Chapter 6. Perhaps that's the next entry point we need to think about for building trust as marketers. But what exactly is a digital bill of rights? What *should* it be? Can we do it on our own? Should we wait for the government to mandate a digital bill of rights before we put the time and money into creating one of our own? Believe me, it will be far more impactful if interested organizations take the initiative to come together on their own and say, "We need to make this better. We can't keep undermining people's trust by not having some clarity around the rules of engagement here."

You can find this now on an individual basis with certain brands. They're the ones who say, "This is our brand promise to you." When you promote a culture in which the customer is always right and that is what the brand promises, it's easy for everyone to understand. However, a lot of brand promises are not easy to understand because we put them out in very arcane terms. And I'm not talking about terms and conditions that get attached to a website—no one reads those, and even fewer people understand them. Maybe the occasional lawyer reads them, but no one else.

I think there might be a first-mover advantage for the company that pioneers a meaningful digital bill of rights. It would be incredibly refreshing if, industry by industry, companies stepped up and drafted their own digital bills of rights for their customers that they are willing to live and die by, and that they will keep repeating until everyone clearly understands where they stand.

I feel we're some distance away from that. It's much easier to declare that you're going to sell quality products and services, and that you're going to strive to make sure customers are satisfied, and you guarantee that if customers are not satisfied with their purchase, they have 30 days to return it.

Big whoop. That's the kind of commercial marketing speak we've been hearing for years—it's not a real bill of rights.

It's not saying we recognize that you, the customers, are the reason for our existence, and as customers, we want to treat you in a way that makes you partners with us in this journey we're hoping you'll take with us. And that's why, if you have this issue, we're going to do this. If you have ideas, we're going to reward you for that. If you help other people, we'll reward you for that too.

One of the things we did in an earlier loyalty program we tested, which seemed to work rather well, is we rewarded people not only for the things they purchased but also for the actions they took on behalf of the brand on their own volition, whether that was writing a review or helping other customers or writing a FAQ answer or whatever it might be. That's something we all should do to build real community.

And what is that value exchange? I don't know what the exchange rate is on that right now, but it's something I think we're going to have to figure out going forward, because people do realize that what's in our heads and what defines us is valuable. It's out there. So how can we make that value equation fair?

The Dark Side of Social

As much as there is to gain from building community and reaching through social channels, there's also a dark side. Almost every large brand has had to deal with the fallout from a customer service issue that goes viral—such as United Airlines, musician Dave Carroll, and the broken Taylor guitar mentioned in Chapter 4. And if an influencer of the magnitude of a Kardashian or Justin Bieber publicly complains about the service they received from your brand, then watch out.

The problem is that while some number of these incidents are triggered by real customers who are dissatisfied with the service they received from a brand, there's no telling if competitors are sometimes poisoning a company's well of digital trust. Recovering from the hit to your reputation can take a long time.

It's one thing to realize your vision for digital trust, but you've also got to defend your vision for digital trust. How you defend it, however, is really important, because you can't defend it the way you used to. Let's say you have a big calamity, such as a data breach or a malware attack. People get upset because every time they hear about that, it suggests that hackers are stealing their personal information and the brand can take a hit. But I think what's important is that while you can't avoid bad things happening, you can preplan for them happening and be prepared not to be defensive, but instead to restore trust and confidence by being clear and quick and proactive. Those are things that brands still struggle with because so many embrace a traditional way of doing PR.

And if you're not firing on all those cylinders, then you're out of luck. You've got to be fast, which suggests that you absolutely must preplan your responses. If I was running a business, I would always assume that at some point my business is going to somehow be attacked digitally. What do you do in that situation? You've got to brainstorm your possible responses up front—what are you going to do, when will you do it, who's going to be involved? I used to call it the "social waterslide." If you've ever been on one of those large amusement park waterslides, once you're on it, you're on it. There's no turning back, no stopping. You're done—everything's automatic once you start to slide and you've got to be prepared to shoot out the other end whether or not you like it.

So, think about contingency planning—what happens immediately in response to an attack, who is part of that exercise, what are the messages you're going to send out to the world, and on what channels will you send them? And before you send out those messages, you've got to have already spent a lot of time thinking about the best messages—ones that are sincere and don't sound trite or—heaven forbid—lame.

The worst thing you can do is act in a way that suggests you've got something to hide or that you don't have your act together. But this happens all the time when brands get caught flat-footed and aren't prepared with carefully thought-out and preapproved messaging. They lose trust. When Amazon charged loyal customer Barbara Carroll shipping costs of $7,543 on an $88 order for three boxes of Pom toilet paper, initially she wasn't concerned. Said Carroll, "As soon as I saw that number I knew I didn't have to worry, because Amazon would see it was a problem and fix it right away."

However, after she tried *six times* to get the shipping charge reversed—even sending an email to company founder

Jeff Bezos—her implicit trust in Amazon understandably became stretched to the limits. According to reports, Amazon's response to her requests was a form message denying a refund because the order "was shipped on time, it was shipped to the right location, and it wasn't damaged." It took an Atlanta-area TV station picking up the story, which quickly went viral, for Amazon to finally reverse the charge more than two months later.[3]

This was an extreme case, but it nonetheless turned a previously happy customer into one who was not so happy, maybe not so loyal or trusting, and the company ended up with a bigger problem than it should have. The issue here was that the processes in place designed to make things work actually got in the way because no one felt empowered to resolve the issue—turning an already absurd situation into a surreal one.

Many businesses and brands today have the same blind spot. They say, "We made the right decision, our processes can't be wrong, we're moving forward, and that's that." But here is an important point: inflexibility and intransigence can undermine trust both for customer and employees. In the Customer Bill of Rights, there is an implicit if not explicit commitment to do the right thing. Unfortunately, that's not always how other people see it. And other people in this case are not necessarily highly leveraged brand personalities or media personalities who have the power to make your life a misery. Everyday people today have access to the entire world—via Facebook, TikTok, Twitter, YouTube, and other platforms—to broadcast what they think about your brand, the good and the bad, 24/7, every day of the week.

So, with that in mind, what do you do?

Part of it is keeping the social waterslide in mind and being ready to immediately address problems the moment they occur. You've got to have at least thought in advance about some of the major issues you're going to encounter over time and what you would do once those events actually come to fruition.

And more important, you need to have your talking points ready to go when bad things happen.

There's nothing worse than being extemporaneous on an extemporaneous platform because you're not thinking, "If I say this, what are the implications? What's the potential blowback? Should I say anything at all?" If you haven't taken the time to prepare in advance, it's usually better to not say anything until you are absolutely sure you know what you're going to do, where it will lead, and how you can bring it to a conclusion. Unfortunately, that's not often the case—instead, we're like deer in the headlights.

So, on one end of the spectrum there's David and Goliath—the influencers with wide reach and considerable pull—and on the other end there are everyday, regular people. All have the power today to hold a brand hostage. We have to be prepared for it. And the way to do that is (1) plan in advance to respond to these problems, (2) have a communication strategy that is ready to be deployed quickly, and (3) designate in advance the people who will be publicly involved in your organization's messaging. And when these things hit, which they inevitably will, anyone else who normally goes out and talks about your company should stay silent about the issue. But—and this is a major but—the number one thing an organization can do to protect against this is to seek to do the right thing in the first place, treating customers and employees as people—people who matter.

That doesn't mean that if someone publicly says, "I think you guys suck," that you shouldn't respond back. More often than not, that is a losing game. If you're engaging directly in that sort of public back-and-forth banter and dialogue, you will lose almost every time. At worst, you look like you're ganging up on some poor individual who was wronged by your big, bad company, and at best, you just look silly. But sometimes, if you are truly authentic and honest you can come out the other end stronger than before.

When actress Roseanne Barr blamed her use of Ambien—a prescription medication for people who have insomnia—for a series of racist tweets, the pill's manufacturer, Sanofi, sent out a tweet of its own:

> *People of all races, religions and nationalities work at Sanofi every day to improve the lives of people around the world. While all pharmaceutical treatments have side effects, racism is not a known side effect of any Sanofi medication.*[4]

And the potentially staid and boring Merriam-Webster responded to complaints that the company was legitimizing LGBTQ people by including the term "genderqueer" in their dictionary with this tweet:

> *People keep*
> *1) saying they don't know what 'genderqueer' means*
> *then*
> *2) asking why we added it to the dictionary*[5]

Once more, this comes back to the importance of building a strong community, because a strong community is the most potent form of defense you can possess when something like this happens. It's far better to have other people—*customers*—coming to your defense, than it is for your PR people to be coming to your defense. It's almost a certain sign of defeat for your PR department to come out and say, "Nothing to see here, we've got it all under control. We did this in response and we're fantastic." Yeah, right. People have become so cynical that no matter what you say, you're going to be in trouble.

But when your loyal customers and influencers leap into the fray, unsolicited, and say, "Wait a minute. I know this company. I know the people. I know what they're doing, and it's not what you're saying—you've got it wrong." If you have enough of that kind of support out in the wild, then that is often enough to put out any fire you've got in social. When you do it the other way around—where your PR department is doing all the messaging—you're often just pouring gasoline on the fire.

Remember: if you're going to talk the talk, you've got to walk the walk. In this day and age, it's not acceptable to just say, "I support this" or "I stand for that," because the next questions you're likely going to get asked are: "Exactly where are you spending the money to do that?" and "How are you doing that?" and "Who's doing that?" and "How are you measuring success against that?"

If, for example, you tell the world that you believe in diversity—it's all over your website, your recruiting media, and your social channels—how many of the people in your C-suite or on your board would actually be classified as diverse? In my opinion most large companies are still struggling with meeting their goals in this area. So, if you're preaching diversity while your C-suite and board lack in diversity, the next question you're going to hear from customers on your social channels is, "Why not?"

How long is it going to take you to recruit a diverse C-suite and board? Are we talking 10 years or 10 weeks? How are you going to use your social channels to engage with your customers and the public to respond to this question and others like them? Some approaches are better than others. It's a good idea to put some serious thought into how you roll out your messaging via your social channels before you do it. The internet never forgets.

The Battle Over Control

One last thing to consider is the battle over control—how much control do you exert over your own business and how much do you cede to your customers? This is a question that is incredibly hard for any business to deal with. My hypothesis would be the more you can democratize and cede power to customers and not just to your shareholders or to your C-suite the better. If customers feel not only that they have been heard, but more important, that you can be relied on to walk the walk when you talk the talk, and that what they say influences how you do business, the more your customers will feel invested in that brand and the more they will feel like they've made a difference. This is true whether it's customers, employees, or vendors.

In my view, if you do it right, there's nothing more liberating and powerful than sharing some of that control and power. It will pay for itself fast, particularly when you think about how some of the better brands will engage with their customers to make their products better. If you just sit in a room by yourself and do not talk with your customers, or just talk with them in passing, you'll get a completely different—and likely false—perspective that has no value. But if you can engage with people in a meaningful way on a regular basis, for every 100 ideas, you're going to get one that's worth half a billion dollars. That's incredibly powerful.

And the same thing goes for marketing. Apple's Shot on iPhone Challenge ad campaign was successful for a variety of reasons. I don't know if it immediately convinced more people to buy iPhones, but I'm certain it made people stop and think about buying an iPhone because people react positively to great imagery. When they see a photo they love, they can't help but wonder how they can take one just like it. And that makes the story come alive and it makes it more personal, and it makes people put themselves in it and therefore become invested in the brand, which I'm certain converts into sales over time.

9

The Value of Promoting Authenticity, Reputation, and Real Engagement

It takes 20 years to build a reputation and 5 minutes to ruin it.

—Warren Buffett

Something I think that gets lost in the fray is spending a lot of time as marketers, as service people, as business leaders, extrapolating what we *think* people want. Unfortunately, we don't often make a real effort to walk in their shoes, meaning, going through the actual process as though you're the customer. And by the way, in our everyday lives, we often *are* the customer. Ironically, we seem to have a kind of convenient amnesia when it comes to this fact. We erroneously believe that we couldn't possibly be providing a terrible experience for our customers because we put so much effort and spend so much money in making the experience great.

But truth be told, the digital experiences we deliver to our customers, employees, and others are in many cases sorely lacking in basic human empathy. They don't allow for the things that we as humans get stuck on, get frustrated by, or simply desire. Instead, we deliver a lot of pain and frustration. That is all the more reason to apply empathetic design to our customer/employee-facing digital systems, humanizing the experience. Let's consider seven ways to do just that.

Be the Customer

If you haven't actually been a customer of the thing that you're trying to sell—a product, a service, whatever it might be—then you shouldn't start any new digital initiatives, especially large, complex, and expensive ones. And I would argue that you shouldn't start the small, simple, and inexpensive ones either.

All design approaches should start with reference to *real* current experiences to identify the moments that matter—what works, what frustrates, what could be better. That, in my view, is the number one way to determine whether your process—or more important, your *experience*—is broken and where to direct your focus to fix it.

We advertisers and marketers have long claimed we were being empathetic when we spitballed ideas in a darkened room, or when we pursued heavy-duty research projects and segmentation. We'd spend anywhere from 8 to 16 weeks conducting quantitative and qualitative surveys spending hours in rooms with focus groups talking to people. That was fine—we'd invariably end up with a lot of insights that we hadn't always anticipated. We could then tease out insights because we had so much data—more than we had even a few years earlier. It was a bit like Moore's Law on steroids.

So, how can we take a step back and start with what that end-to-end experience is, including all the things that go wrong? We always tend to assume everything is going to go right, and of course that's rarely the case. Do this, and people will buy that. Put an item in the cart, and we've got something that will pop up and tell the customer there's another product they might want to buy to go with what's in the cart. We do those kinds of things, and we think we're done and can move on to the next challenge.

Not by a long shot.

In truth, what we've done only provides flat processes and experiences that go nowhere because they're not truly empathetic. They don't take into consideration that maybe, 4 times out of 10, someone makes a mistake in ordering, and here's what that looks like. And by the way, we make it really hard for them to fix that mistake without having to jump through a whole bunch of hoops. Or they can't find something, and they quit the site in frustration.

How can you really know what customers go through if you aren't experiencing your site for yourself as a customer? I personally make a point of doing this. When I start a new engagement with a new client, in almost every case, I begin the engagement by visiting the client's site and pretending I'm a customer—experiencing what customers go through, both the good and the bad.

For the longest time, I thought we could apply our analytic methods and tools, look at the data, see what the behavior is, and then divine what is actually going on without taking a step back—that is, going through the process end to end and notating what that felt like, and what went right and what went wrong. That was a mistake.

Now, I start every client interaction with, "I actually shopped your site—the content is confusing," or "I couldn't find an item because this link was circuitous," or "When I went to buy something and I made a mistake, I couldn't easily fix it and that was frustrating," or "You gave me something that took four weeks when I thought it would only take seven days, and you didn't tell me in any meaningful way through messaging how to manage my expectations."

I see it time and time again, even with organizations that are really good at building some pretty decent experiences. They still get some of this stuff wrong, and I can't help but think that it's because they didn't put themselves in their customers' shoes. I will sit down with a PowerPoint and show a client—without even using a finger on a keyboard for coding—what I think a good experience might be. We go here next, click that, and just animate it. The decks turn out to be very long, but they do help me and my clients visualize what things could be, where those moments that matter are, and what you might need to do to get over those.

And that's the big piece here; you've got to go through it, you've got to be the customer—even when you're serving somebody else. But, explains Ragy Thomas, founder and CEO of Sprinklr:

> *It's not going to happen because somebody mandates it, it's going to happen because there's an enabling piece of technology and the company shifts its thinking. So, two things have to happen. One, is the company has to go from brand-centric to customer-centric. And two, there has to be an enabling piece of technology that allows you to go from brand centricity to customer centricity. And every CEO who doesn't become customer-centric will be replaced by a CEO who is customer-centric. We're talking about a 10-to-20-year transformation, at the end of which we look radically different.*

I might suggest that customer-centrism is not enough—brands need to become life-centric and strive to understand the context of their customer's journey as much as the immediate need.

John Legere, the former CEO of T-Mobile, was famous for having a phone line installed in his office specifically so he could listen in on customer service calls. Not just once or twice a month, or even once or twice a week, but often for three hours a day. In this way, he could hear for himself what T-Mobile's customers had on their minds—the good, but most often the bad (it was a customer service line, after all).

While Legere's approach was a step in the right direction, it didn't really get to the heart of the customer experience.

The twist on that is going full force and *being* the customer, because that changes your perspective from "I can look at things and see that some of our customers are frustrated," to "Now I can really feel what it's like being one of our customers." There's a big difference between those two perspectives.

Knowing what it feels like is visceral, and it's the visceral feelings I find to be the most empowering because we're humans. And as humans, in many cases, we act because of the visceral and emotional feelings we experience. What we often do to be practical and tactical about it is create storyboards for the walk-the-mile piece. Show people what happens next, where the inflection points are—the moments that matter. A customer can't get what they want in the time they want because they can't find it. Consider what would happen if you sent someone an invitation, but then you made it hard for them to buy or research the thing you invited them to buy.

Understand What Data Is Sufficient to Drive That Improved Experience

What are the things that would make the experience better for your customers? For your employees? What would you have to do to get the right concept, the right person, at the right time? There's a whole raft of things that would enable that, starting with data. What data would you need to act? We consider these questions day in and day out, but we don't necessarily do it through the lens of empathy. We instead do it through the lens of process, or expediency, or efficiency, or what we think people absolutely need but nothing else. That gives us the minimum threshold to get something done.

So, let's say you've identified five moments that matter in the entire story for a customer, what data is *just enough* to make something happen? Do you have to collect more? Can you divine it from other things that are part of the organization? How do you knit that together so that suddenly, you have an equation that actually causes something to happen? That's one of the hardest things to do because what is *just enough*? Gene Cornfield explains that the eternal thirst for more data is often driven by chief marketing officers (CMOs). Says Gene:

The reality is that almost all CMOs are data-driven, it just depends on what data they're driven by. I have a little illustration called the CMO Brain that I did as a joke and shared with a few people.

My illustration shows the most primitive right-brained CMO, I call the Chief Makeover Officer. What's the natural thing you do as a CMO when you're new in your role? You change the brand—it's "We need a new brand." They measure things like brand health and brand perception. These CMOs are driven by data, but it's typically about the brand.

A somewhat less-primitive, but still largely right-brained CMO, is the Chief Media Officer. They're concerned with reach, frequency, and awareness. They're still measuring things, but what they're measuring has more to do with media.

Then you start getting into left-brained CMOs. You have the Chief Metrics Officer who typically didn't grow up in agencies—they might not have even been marketers and their company might not even value marketing. You find this a lot in B2B. They're looking at leads generated, MQLs, SQLs, multitouch attribution, and maybe revenue. The focus is usually on more business data, less marketing data—or marketing data and business data.

You then have probably the most advanced left-brained CMO, which I refer to as the Chief Manipulation Officer. How do I learn so much about you that I can get you to do what I want? How do I ingest from social, and all these third party and second party sources, to build my customer 360, to get you to optimize for the outcomes I care about? I want to get you the right offer, but it's not about what you want, it's about how I can best manipulate you to do what I want.

And then you have the highly advanced right-brained CMO, the Chief Meaning Officer. They ask: "How do I understand what's important to you? How do I measure how well my team, my company, is actually performing for what's important to you?" They recognize that when people achieve a purpose important to them, they generate value for whichever company enabled them to do so. Sometimes that value is revenue, sometimes that value is share of spend. Sometimes it's lifetime value, sometimes it's market share, sometimes it's retention. But realize that all those growth-oriented metrics that the company cares about, every single one of them is a byproduct of a customer achieving something important to them, something meaningful to them.

The Chief Meaning Officer doesn't ignore business metrics, doesn't ignore marketing metrics. But their primary focus is on: "How do I measure what's important to my customers? Because logic says the better that an organization performs on the expectations, or outcomes important to its customers, the better those customers will perform on the outcomes important to the business."

Usually, when we think about all the data we need to get the job done, we tend to go overboard—the equivalent of "We'll get a triple-cheeseburger with large side of fries and a jumbo chocolate shake with whipped cream and a cherry on top." But when we get all that data, we're overwhelmed by it and that slows down the process.

But if you turn it around and ask, "To create a human experience with *just* enough data, what is that 'just' bit, and can we be much lighter in general as we create these triggers across the experience that we're trying to create?" And that is an interesting question. Consider the example of chatbots. More often than not, when an organization creates a chatbot and they put it out in the wild, people get frustrated because it doesn't do everything that they thought it would do. The problem is you're not actually talking to a human, you're talking to an algorithm, and an algorithm is not sentient.

So, what do you do?

Chatbots and other forms of technology are in many ways like children. To humanize them, you have to put them in a nursery and teach them. And you need a team that's designed to not just look at the data, but to look at how people are using it, and what they're getting—or not getting—out of the questions they ask. When you do that, you might find it necessary to change everything you've done and start from the ground up.

Understand What Technology Is Needed to Enable the Experience

As marketers, we may think we need a CDP (customer data platform), or some form of data repository, or a CMS (content management system). You name it, there's technology out there to meet most any need.

The fact of the matter is we get caught up in implementing really big platform decisions that could enable a whole raft of great experiences. But the problem is that people often aren't thinking about the contextual, human element here. Instead, they're thinking about things such as: How can I get more throughput through these systems? How can I take data and move it from one place to another? How can I create a campaign real fast? How can I customize content in an email and send it out? How can I trigger an event in an online experience?

What is needed is a CEP—*customer experience platform*—but not a whole new set of technologies. A CEP is more a state of mind and set of organizing principles utilizing the data and technologies you may already have in a way that that supports those moments that matter to your customers. Gene Cornfield offers an example of a situation in which the technology exists to create those customer moments that matter but are not being used effectively:

> *One day, I had the response to a client RFP due at noon. I was on the Acela train from Boston to New York, and we all know that Wi-Fi on the Acela is not always reliable. In fact, that day it was out. So, I tethered my laptop to my phone and there I was trying to upload this 10 MB document.*
>
> *Partway through the upload, I received a text on my phone from my provider. The text said something like, "You've hit your bandwidth threshold for the month and we're now throttling your bandwidth back to some pitifully slow speed."*

"What?" I thought to myself. "Why aren't you asking me? Give me the option to either say, 'Sure, fine,' or 'No, I'll pay for more bandwidth.'" In that situation—with the clock quickly ticking down on my deadline—of course I'll pay for more.

As I was waiting for the file to upload, I could tell it was going nowhere fast. So, I was faced with a decision: should I cancel the upload and risk the client not getting it? Instead, I went to the app on my phone. I searched for the place to change my data plan, but the search was going extremely slow too. "I can't even change my data plan!"

I abandoned the app and called my provider. Before I was put on hold, I got the happy recording, "Did you know you could do most things in our app?" Not if you throttle my bandwidth, I can't! I finally get through to somebody, and they said, "Hi, this is so and so, how can I help you?"

"How do you not know how you can help me?" I asked, incredulous. "You just throttled my bandwidth 10 minutes ago—you should know that. And then I went to the app to try to change my data plan—you should know that. Why are you asking me?"

I'm sure the person on the other end of the phone was thinking that I was an insane person. They were probably thinking, "I've never talked to you in my life, how would I know that?" My expectation was that provider as an entity should have recognized these interactions that I had with the company. And right or wrong, the human expectation is that I would've been heard, and you would remember our prior interactions. It's a very human expectation.

Actually, our expectation as humans is that corporations are people— they're entities. Our relationship with a company, from the company's point of view, might be the sum total of our transactions. But that's not how we as humans measure a relationship.

Unfortunately, organizations don't always think about how marketing flows directly into service or sales or commerce and back again. And the moments that matter across each could be so much better if brands took some time to think about the transitions, where information flows—how information *should* flow— based on the behaviors, but more important, based on the contextual knowledge you have of the customer.

Again, that's a new frontier that few organizations have had tremendous success with to date. And even the ones that have some pretty powerful algorithms that could say, "If you bought this, customers like you buy that." You only have to remove one piece of data, such as who's on the account at the moment, for that whole system to fall apart. Plus, you're talking about proxies—just because I bought this right now doesn't mean I'll buy something else tomorrow. I was in the context of something, and now I'm not. And so, why would I?

Years ago, traditional marketers using segmentation would say the same thing. These segments are somewhat immobile. You do a ton of work, and you find the three out of five segments that are going to be the most receptive to your marketing campaigns, or your new product or service launch, or whatever it may be, because they have these characteristics. So, all we need to do is go and find people in our various databases—internal and external—with the same characteristics and use the technology that we've got to do that.

Again, what happens is that people assume these things are immutable, that they are fixed. And in truth, I believe that segments are not fixed. They're as fluid as context will allow.

Just because I'm painting my house today doesn't mean that I need a roomful of new home decor tomorrow. It may be just this isolated event, and you just needed to understand where I was in that. But, next time, maybe you can anticipate where I'm going. And that's the thing—most marketing is still, even today, very rearview mirror. We're looking at and analyzing the past, not seeing into the future. The technology's there, but it's not getting selected and applied wisely, and it's not being used in the most effective way.

The idea of minimum viable product (MVP) is common in software product development. According to Eric Ries, author of *Lean Startup*, this is the version of a new product that allows a team to collect the maximum amount of validated learning about customers with the least amount of effort. Instead of creating some massive system or process that does every possible thing in the world, and maybe a bit more, just create something that does the one thing you need done in service to the customer.

I have an ongoing debate about this with Grad Conn,[1] former CMO of Sprinklr. My position was that when it comes to making investments in technology, companies need to be a lot nimbler and more agile. Grad's standpoint was different because I think he's at a point now where a lot of his clients are saying, "We need to figure out how this all scales. If we can't figure that out, if we can't go big, then go home." That's a different side of the coin I often hear, which is, "I've made these major investments in technologies, but I don't feel like I'm getting the value I need out of them."

Again, it's a visceral or gut feeling. And the reason is that the transparency isn't there in terms of assessing what it is that success looks like and what return you're expecting up-front. A lot of these things occur because we're comparing different platforms with one another based on their features and functions versus their desired business impact. But then the folks who make those decisions don't necessarily always go down the path of saying, "By the way, if I'm spending $10 million on this platform, I need to make a $100 million back over the next 18 to 24 months." And that's the challenge.

So when Grad says, "Actually, I think we need to be able to figure out how to scale sooner," he is right. We need to move beyond small bite-sized entrepreneurial gestures. We need to push ourselves to figure out now how to make money from these investments from the start—be bold or go home. How do we justify the expense that we've made? That's one way of looking at it.

But that still doesn't necessarily negate the need to get something done. Maybe again, the word *context* is important here, which is, depending on the context and where you are in the business cycle and what you're trying to do determines whether you push for scale from the start or iterate toward the end goal. Doing something is far better than doing nothing and waiting for the perfect storm of things to occur together so that you could scale something. But we should absolutely have a path to scaling baked in when we're thinking of doing this kind of digital transformation.

Which takes us back to the moments that matter.

You've got to put a price tag on the moments that matter. Let's say you got to a sticking point with a customer because they couldn't find the parts they needed. They found the SKU eventually, but it was hard for them on the commerce side. So they took that SKU, they put it in Google, and they found the item faster or for less cost someplace else. That is a moment that matters. That is an inflection point. They would have gone with you, but you made it hard for them to complete the transaction, so they went with someone else.

The thought was you take that and then you say, "Let's build a business case around it. We'll build a business case around the moment that matters in an experience that's important." And that's the thing we put a price tag on. It might, for example, be worth $500 million in additional incremental parts sales. Well, what greater motivation could you have to make an investment than to know that if you do it right, you're going to make 5 times or 10 times more on it? And that's the lens we must use when we consider technology.

Measure Value Drivers

The number one question I get asked by clients is this: How can I understand the real value I should be getting from these data and technology investments? Measuring value drivers is a key part of empathetic design. Without this piece, even the most people-centric system falls apart. Without this piece, the walking-a-mile in your customers' shoes stuff is all touchy-feely and it doesn't have much obvious measurable impact. Without this piece, you can suck up all the data you want, but you're not going to use it for anything, a lot of it's just going to fall on the floor. It's like the classic *I Love Lucy* episode I mentioned in Chapter 3, where Lucy and her best friend Ethel dropped more and more chocolates on the shop floor (and stuffed into their mouths and clothing) as the boss kept increasing the speed of the conveyor belt.

Without this piece, you might make tech investments that on paper look like good choices at the time, but I guarantee you two or three years from now—if you're even around and running the program—someone's going to tap you on the shoulder and ask, "You know, we spent $10 million on this. Did we make $100 million on it? $200 million? $500 million? Did we make *anything* from that investment?"

Most people will scratch their heads and answer with a blank stare because they've moved on long ago. That's the thing. This value piece must be in place *now*, not later. If we're a data-driven, experience-based company, then the value drivers include the data, the technology, the human, emotional, and visceral empathetic stuff, and the lens. The lens is the financial return on our investment—is it going to give us a return? If so, how quickly? If not, should we be doing something different?

Which leads us to the next question: How should we measure the lens—the financial return on our investment?

Generally, you would do this in the same way you would if you were starting a business or any other venture. You would ask questions along the lines of: Who's my market? What's the nature of demand? What's it going to take to deliver on that demand? What's the market share I can expect to get? What additional considerations do I need to make in terms of having to get out there and market the things we're selling? And then, what's left over?

That's your return on investment—you put this money in, and you get that money out.

In many ways, I don't think that's mutable. It doesn't change—it's what you do. But few organizations go this far; they don't take it to the level of thinking about the moments that matter and putting a business case around that. It's a microbusiness case, and that's the thing that's often missing.

I think about Capital One as the ultimate analytic company. The thing that's amazing about them—and it's still as true today as it was 10 or 15 years ago when I knew them—is that they made a real commitment that everyone in the company is going to be extremely analytically oriented. They can take a blank piece of paper, without having done a ton of work just yet, and do a quick back of the envelope to tell you whether a new card product is going to have any value for the company whatsoever. And then they'll go and do the heavy lifting later. Anyone in Capital One has the ability to measure the value drivers, and they do.

Iterate Often

The human journey is a learning process, and none of us should think that we'll ever be done with it. Despite our best efforts or our deepest fantasies, it's never going to be "Okay, I stood up this platform and now I hand over the keys—I'm done." That's neither a realistic nor a smart outcome.

As part of the value framework we create, there needs to be an educational learning component that in effect states, "We got 80 percent of the way there, but now we need to be very structured and apply the same process to make sure that we are adapting, and the investments are adapting, in a way that makes them better every week." Otherwise, it'll just be, "Okay—let's wait until the next code freeze, and then we'll ..."

Customers don't care about your code freeze. What the customer *does* care about is trying to use their credit card to complete a purchase but can't because your form encryption isn't functioning correctly, leaving 10 percent of your customers who can't buy *anything* using their favorite browser. It happens more often than you might think, and you probably don't even know about it. You might instead think the problem is a result of abandoned carts.

These are living systems that are in a state of constant flux and change. Making improvements on them must be a structured, iterate-often process. And then, whether it's mystery shopping every two weeks, or every month, or whatever, seeing what it *feels* like combined with the empirical data that you're getting from the behavior of your customers or employees—that's where it gets interesting.

The same goes for content. Organizations create content and they have creators of content, but they don't always think about the *curators* of content that can market the content. I think, if you have a huge content organization, it needs to be more like a media company than like a content-origination company.

Make no mistake, creating structured, iterate-often processes is a commitment, but it's a necessary one to find the success you seek.

So iterate often. You're always learning, always improving. You're never done.

Build an Empathetic Organization

Your organization is only as strong as its weakest link. And right now, we're still in the mode of keeping our operations somewhat distinct and separate. Someone always has responsibility. There's the CMO for marketing, there are corporate communications, there's the service team, there's the manufacturing team, there's the sales team, and so on. But today, more than ever before, these functions are blurring together.

If you're a CIO, you need to be aware of and think like a marketer or a salesperson, and not just treat these groups as clients. And vice versa, if you are a CMO, you need to be not just empathetic, but familiar and comfortable using, diagnosing, and specifying technology and data.

The correct answer is not, "I'm the CMO, let me go out and get an agency."

The best organizations have CMOs who are conversant in analytics, technology, digital, and most important, in empathetic design. Imagine if your entire C-suite was able to think that way, and they might not have to be all smooshed together and whatever, but they could navigate those transitions between the various groups better, more effectively.

Ultimately, empathy is key. Explains Sprinklr's Ragy Thomas:

> *You need to have emotional empathy. You need to be passively intimate. All this will come back to: Do you have the ability to know the customer in real time? Do you have the ability to listen to that customer in real time? Do you have the ability to work across all your faculties to do the best? We have a framework that we call "Listen, Learn, Love," which is really the foundation of Sprinklr. The ability to listen to your customers, the ability to learn from what your customers tell you. What is it that matters to you? Who are you? What are you trying to say to me? What is the issue? And then, showing love for your customers across all your silos. Can I show you that I care across every digital and non-digital touchpoint? That is the key.*

Use the Trust Index to Measure Brand Health

The health of your brand is something you should measure externally and internally on a regular basis. Why? Because there is a direct correlation between your overall brand health and your ability to accomplish the business plan that you put forth. This, to me, is the linchpin.

As people have moved more and more to modern channels versus traditional digital channels such as websites, that creates a whole raft of new expectations. If you are conducting conversational commerce, you'd better be authentic and able to extend the brand promise to that experience at that moment in that context.

One way of doing that or making sure is that you put all those channels and all those motions and operations through a lens of, are we building trust here? Are we building the relationship in some fashion? It doesn't have to be a palsy relationship where you're constantly talking with the customer 24/7. A relationship can be anything. It should just be an affinity for the brand, and it's top of mind when you have a need, but maybe you don't always have that need. It evaporates quickly if you violate the trust equation.

So what is the trust equation?

$$\text{Value} = \text{Authenticity} \times \text{Knowledge} / \text{Sentiment}$$

It's one part figuring out how your company becomes more authentic—its employees, customers, and vendors.

Multiply that with what you know about them. Tell me three things about your most valuable customer your competitors don't know.

Then, divide by how that customer is feeling about you at any given time, because what you know about them and how you project yourself with them goes to what kind of sentiment and affinity that customer is going to have for you.

10

Power Sharing and the Human Experience—The Next Wave of Growth

The creative people I admire seem to share many characteristics: A fierce restlessness. Healthy cynicism. A real-world perspective.

An ability to simplify. Restraint. Patience. A genuine balance of confidence and insecurity. And most importantly, humanity.

—David Droga

It's not a bad thing to talk about humanizing digital, to consider it, to kick it around. But to gain the tremendous power that it can unleash in your organization and for your customers and your employees, at some point you need to do more than talk. You need to act. And once you act, you may have to create a situation where there's no going back.

Throughout history, military commanders have used the tactic of burning bridges (or boats) to prevent their troops from retreating—thus increasing their motivation to succeed in battle. With the bridge gone, there was no going back. And that's the thing I think a lot of marketers have a hard time navigating. They often say they want to create a better experience for their customers, but when the going gets tough, they forget all about it and retreat over the bridge—returning to their familiar, tried-and-true ways of doing business.

What we're trying to do, however, is build bridges to something *different* and then burn down the old ones. That's a hard thing for many people to do. But there is real, measurable value to be gained that can make the difference between a brand that survives and one that doesn't. And this is directly related to your willingness and ability to take technology and use it for a more intimate and relevant contextual experience.

That's what we call human. And I believe that those who get it right are going to be the successful ones in the next 5 to 10 years, while those who keep doing what they're doing on the old islands will be stuck there, and that's a hard lesson to learn.

In the preceding chapters, I have provided you with a variety of tactics and strategies you can readily apply to humanize digital in your organization. Now, I would like to step back and consider the big picture of what you can and should be doing right now. You'll recognize some of these things from earlier in the book, and others appear only in this chapter. In any case, I suggest that this roadmap will help you get where you want to go without having to retreat to the familiar and comfortable island you've been living on for so long.

Three Things

First, if you do nothing else today, take a piece of paper—an index card, a notebook, or fire up your computer—and write down three things you know about your most valuable customer that your competitors do not. Not 10 things, not one thing—three things. That's the best place for anyone to start.

If you *can't* make a list of just three things, then you've got a problem. It's a sure sign that don't know the customer, you don't know what they're thinking, you don't know what's unique about them, and you don't know what your most valuable customers' trigger points are. Ahead of anything else, this is what you most need to know—and fast.

So what if you can't come up with three things—what then?

Ask yourself, "What are my customers telling me?" It's not just how much data you have, it's what motivates your customers that is truly meaningful? Here's a hypothetical example of Apple. What three things do you think motivate Apple customers the most to keep people buying their products? Using my own family as an example, we've bought somewhere in the neighborhood of six Apple laptops over the past 15 years or so, and we've bought seven or eight Apple iPhones.

Why do we keep coming back?

In the case of laptops, it's not because there aren't capable Windows-based computers—there are. HP, LG, Dell, Asus, and others all make highly reviewed machines. In some cases, they're faster, with larger screens and more memory and storage for a lot less money than the equivalent Apple products. Regardless, we still buy Apple laptops.

And in the case of smartphones, it's not because Samsung, Motorola, Google, and others don't make good products; they do. And it's also not because our cellular service provider, AT&T, prefers that we buy Apple smartphones. They offer a variety of different smartphones to customers that work just fine on the AT&T network. Regardless, we still buy Apple iPhones.

So why do we keep coming back?

It's because Apple's customer experience makes us want to come back. We're motivated by design, and Apple clearly puts a lot of thought, effort, and money into creating great product designs. And Apple's design aesthetic goes far beyond its gorgeous products—it pervades the entire brand and everything it touches. Their creativity is really well thought out, reflecting their design aesthetic, and so are the Apple retail stores.

Whenever I go into an Apple Store, I have the feeling that they're really on top of their game. They greet me at the door, if there's a queue they get me on the waiting list, and I'm welcome to play with their display products while I'm waiting. Apple's salespeople are super knowledgeable, and they have great technical support available via their Genius Bar. While Apple may not have pioneered this kind of customer experience, they for sure now own it. When I step into an Apple Store, I know what to expect and I feel good about it. It hits me emotionally as well as practically.

Think about your own brand for a moment. Does it have the kind of emotional appeal that attracts people and converts them into loyal customers for the long run? What is it about your product—or the way you deliver it—that triggers your loyal customers to stay that way? If you hope to succeed in the long run, you must establish an emotional connection with customers that is very deep.

I have a deep, emotional connection to Apple and its products. The high quality I want is there, and that quality is extended to every touchpoint I've ever engaged with. I therefore don't mind giving Apple my business. In fact, I like doing it. But if in the future they start to deviate too much from what I expect from the brand, or if they disappoint me, then that leaves an opportunity for another company to try to earn my business and my loyalty as a customer. You might be a company that has found the secret to delivering great service, but if you get complacent, then you could find that your customers aren't there any longer.

The Aging Generation

There's a large group of people who are fast becoming one of the key segments for marketers, particularly in technology. I'm not talking about Gen Xers, Millennials, or Gen Zers. The group I'm talking about is the aging population, specifically Boomers and older, and there are enormous opportunities within this group right now.

Think about your own family for a moment and how everyone has a story about being the IT call center for their mom or dad. We've all experienced that—I know I have. What's driving this is because brands haven't always kept the human in mind when they design and sell and support them. And they definitely haven't kept older people in mind.

Do these people need lots of bells and whistles? No. Do they have trouble hearing, seeing? Yes, they do. It's hard. Older people often can't see what they're supposed to be doing, therefore it's frustrating and it appears they're not technically minded when they really are.

So, when you think about this group in particular, what are the three most valuable things they would be willing to pay for? More than any other group, older people will be willing to pay for products and services that make their lives simpler and easier. You could build a whole system: people would happily pay for the IT service required to keep their smartphone, their laptop, their desktop, and smart devices in their homes—their alarm system, video doorbell, Wi-Fi-enabled thermostat, and so on—working together properly.

Making that really easy for this demographic could pay enormous dividends, but no one seems to be intersecting with that right now. Companies just put their products out there, and if customers need help, they can go find an online manual or maybe their kids will help them out. That to me is the poster child for the lack of human-driven experiences and thinking about the human first.

The Post-COVID Organization

Again, start with the experience, start with the human, start with an understanding that we are all going through this journey and this brief experiment called life. Being able to use technology to make those lives better is the core of purpose. It's not selling more shaving foam or more cars or more Caribbean vacations. It's, "I want to make your life a little easier, a little better. And I want you to know that you matter to me as a customer, and I want you to know that you matter to me as an employee."

Which brings us back to the fact that humanizing digital doesn't just apply to our customers, but also to our employees and to our organizations. It's our people who also must deal with the digital decisions we've made, and those decisions are often not good ones. When we lose good employees—frustrated or thwarted by the decisions we've made—the destruction of value is incalculable. We must treat our people as humans, not as resources. That's really got to change.

As we deal with the aftermath of the COVID-19 pandemic, we're coming out of a watershed moment during which we've been forced to use technology in ways we've never even considered. When businesses shut down and people started working from home in greatly increased numbers, we used technology to help keep employees, teams, and entire organizations together—remotely.

While I expect that we will one day return to a semblance of the pre-COVID world that we are still familiar with, we have learned some valuable lessons through the ordeal. We've learned that we can be productive and work together and collaborate and innovate, even when we're not in a room together. Before COVID, most businesspeople thought you had to physically be together in the same room to get important things done. That, of course, is one of the most common and most human feelings we possess—to want to be together. We need and thrive on live social interaction.

So the question is, what's the balance?

There are seminal moments that change the course of history—good, bad, or otherwise—whether it's the result of humans or something else. It could be war, famine, disease, volcanoes, hurricanes, a wayward asteroid—any number of things.

Those moments force us to move forward a lot faster than we would normally go as a species. For decades, we'll just cruise along, making incremental changes in terms of what we do. And then suddenly something hits us that we can't ignore, and everything changes, and it changes a lot. COVID-19 caused us to skip forward a lot further and a lot faster than what typically happens in the normal progression of human history.

When the Black Death—bubonic plague, caused by the bacterium *Yersinia pestis* and primarily spread by fleas carried by rodents—ravaged the world during the fourteenth century, an estimated 75 million people died. Like COVID-19, the plague was indiscriminate in the victims it chose. Rich, poor, male, female, young old—*Y pestis* didn't care. Entire villages were decimated, and populations wiped out. However, the Black Death was especially prevalent in densely populated cities where people with the disease were in close proximity to those who didn't yet have it, and it most often killed people who were already frail or unwell—who had preexisting conditions.

Historians believe that the Black Death had tremendous and long-lasting effects on humanity. With so many deaths, there was a big labor shortage, putting extreme strain on the feudal system of lords (who owned the land) and serfs (who worked the land). To attract and retain laborers, the lords had to improve pay and working conditions for the serfs. Years later, after the Black Death abated and lords tried to roll back these changes, the serfs rebelled—retaining many of their gains. In addition, when people realized that priests and prayers and church services didn't have the power to stop the Black Death, many turned away from religion altogether.[1]

The Black Death changed the way we worked, it changed the way we lived, and it changed the way we interacted with one another. And it even changed us physically to a certain degree because people who were genetically stronger and naturally more resistant to the plague bacterium were able to survive and pass on their genes to their children, who were then able to pass on their genes to *their* children. Society as a whole moved forward much faster after the Black Death than it had in the years preceding it.

I think this is the kind of moment we're experiencing today, when things just slip forward a lot faster than we ever imagined possible. We all thought, sure, online commerce—Amazon and all the rest—is going to be the thing that we gravitate toward. Little did we know that it was not going to just be a B2C thing, but it was going to be a B2B thing. Everybody's expecting that sort of model of being able to get something without requiring a lot of effort and "administrivia." They're all expecting the same experience, and that has opened up new opportunities that didn't exist even a few years ago.

Big-box retailers were putting thousands of mom-and-pop shops out of business, but now it's coming full circle. Smaller, more agile businesses are gaining ground as they adapt and apply technology very quickly using minimal resources. You don't have to spend tens of thousands of dollars to put out a shingle and start getting business—you can do that overnight. And it also opens up the desire, because we have taken all the commoditized stuff that we don't like doing, and it's given us this new dimension where you can do things like pick up your groceries at the store without getting out of your car—"Just put it in the back, I don't want to even talk to anyone."

There's a greater focus in my view, and there will continue to be a greater focus in my view, on better experiences when we do get together. And I believe that is true, not only in terms of being together with customers but also in terms of being together with your employees and with your colleagues. The game has slipped forward to the point where you'd better bring along more interesting elements, because when you do get together, it's got to be really high quality. Says Peter Smith:

> *Your company's growth comes down to how good of an experience you can create, and I think that companies for a long time have talked about things like personalization in very handwavy terms. They don't get into*

what's driving us, what's motivating us, what our purpose is in searching for a particular product.

My mom was trying to buy a laptop from a large online computer retailer. She went to their website, saw something she liked, and clicked on the listing. That click took her into the product detail page where she was presented with basically a parts catalog of dropdowns to select from—like a bunch of pick lists.

"Okay," she thought to herself, "512 MB, 1 TB, 2 TB, SSD, VME, HDD. I have no idea what to do." She clicked the information icon a few times to try to get translations for all these techy acronyms and terms, and she tried to engage a chatbot on the site. The net result was she ended up getting frustrated. She didn't feel confident spending $2,000 because this was all just far too complicated for her. She abandoned the transaction.

And how did the computer retailer respond to that? "Let me target her." They sent her a ton of emails with promotional offers to try to close her. But at no point in that process did they look at the indicator—that she clicked an information icon three or four times and tried to engage a chatbot—and deduce that she wanted more information to get comfortable about her purchase. She wasn't debating whether or not to purchase. She just didn't feel comfortable selecting from those dropdowns.

So even simple things like that, companies do a horrible job today of tapping into the 99.9 percent of data they have available to them to better serve a customer's purpose or intent. Instead, when given the option of picking between relevancy and reach, they're picking reach 100 percent of the time. Just because it's cheap, it's easy, and you can use email templates. But the result is you're not developing a relationship with your consumer, and you're undermining their trust in your brand—their sense that you understand them, and their belief that you actually care about what's best for them as opposed to the next transaction for that company.

We used to come together because we *had* to come together—let's set up a meeting. I always joke, why are meetings always in half-hour and one-hour increments? Do we really need to set aside that exact amount of time? What usually happens is, when someone sets up a half-hour meeting, we use the time, whether or not we need to. When someone sets up a one-hour meeting, we use the time. But did we use the time effectively? Was it high quality?

I think where we're going to go is toward scoring the quality of time that we're spending together in terms of innovation. We move something, we change something, we make something happen in this half hour or 15 minutes. It was born out of the internet bubble where people wanted to interact and collaborate in different ways than they had been used to in corporate America. And incentivize people to bring creativity into the spotlight. Organizations that can't do that are not going to get and keep great talent. The right talent is going to gravitate toward places where, when we come together and have a meeting, it's great. They come away thinking, "Wow, that was really good."

We do quality assurance meetings routinely at Accenture. I don't know that I'm particularly good at it, but during a recent meeting, I asked questions that weren't necessarily tactically oriented around a contract *per se* but on the client, specifically in terms of expectations. I simply asked if the team really understood what the client would consider successful at the end of the day. What was each stakeholder expecting both from the project and on a personal level? One of the people who attended the meeting called me afterward and said, "Hey, that was the best Q&A session I've ever had."

I couldn't figure out why, because again, I don't think I'm so great at this. But the reason she said that she was happy about it was because she felt as though she got pushed to learn something about the motivations of the client as a human, and then something clicked. I just think that our brains are getting rewired, and the expectation is that we're not just going to do rubber-stamp stuff and "administrivia," or have a meeting to have another meeting. I think everyone wants to move things forward and feel like they've had impact.

The people element is both a tremendous challenge and opportunity. Steve Jobs once said:

> *Some people say, "Give the customers what they want," but that's not my approach. Our job is to figure out what they're going to want before*

they do. I think Henry Ford once said, "If I'd asked customers what they wanted, they would've told me, 'A faster horse!'" People don't know what they want until you show it to them. That's why I never rely on market research. Our task is to read things that are not yet on the page.

I don't think Jobs meant that you shouldn't listen to your customers because they don't know what they want. Rather, by listening, observing, and learning every day, and by taking note of the challenges, frustrations, and interests that drive us as humans, we might be able to better serve our customers and better anticipate the changing nature of customer needs. The sensitivity to sensing that demand is directly correlated to engaging with customers and employees and shifting the balance of power to better understand what they are telling you.

As Victoria Morrissey explains: "Really listen and say, 'Let me help you find a way to solve your problem that also benefits the company.' One of the best pieces of advice I ever got in my life was something my mother said to me many years ago: 'You have two ears and one mouth, and you should use them proportionately.'"

Organizations that follow this path will build healthy and profitable businesses that are truly of the people, by the people, and for the people. And these businesses will continue to grow and endure for many years to come.

Notes

Introduction

1. https://www.cdc.gov/nchs/data/hus/2010/022.pdf
2. https://www.accenture.com/_acnmedia/Thought-Leadership-Assets/ PDF-3/Accenture-Interactive-Business-of-Experience-Full-Report.pdf

Chapter 2

1. https://s2.q4cdn.com/299287126/files/doc_financials/annual/2001 annualreport.pdf
2. http://www.searsarchives.com/history/annual_reports/2000annual report.pdf
3. Copyright Accenture 2022
4. J.M. Wallace-Hadrill, *The Vikings in Francia*, Stenton Lecture (1974).
5. https://www.nytimes.com/2012/02/19/magazine/shopping-habits.html
6. Ibid.
7. Ibid.

Chapter 3

1. https://www.accenture.com/us-en/insights/strategy/employee-experience
2. https://hbr.org/2014/10/the-value-of-keeping-the-right-customers
3. https://www.benefitnews.com/news/avoidable-turnover-costing-employers-big
4. https://hbr.org/sponsored/2018/02/3-principles-disney-uses-to-enhance-customer-experience

Chapter 4

1. https://www.businessinsider.com/mad-men-v-reality-compare-don-drapers-ads-with-those-that-actually-ran-in-the-1960s-2012-3#but-this-real-samsonite-ad-from-1964-emphasizes-the-style-of-the-luggage-and-not-the-strength-although-previous-campaigns-had-showcased-the-products-strength-18
2. https://www.smithsonianmag.com/innovation/texting-isnt-first-new-technology-thought-impair-social-skills-180958091/
3. https://www.accenture.com/us-en/blogs/technology-innovation/carrel-billiard-cooperative-experiences
4. https://www.mcafee.com/blogs/privacy-identity-protection/key-findings-from-our-survey-on-identity-theft-family-safety-and-home-network-security/
5. https://www.slicktext.com/blog/2019/02/survey-consumer-privacy-fears-after-cambridge-analytica/
6. https://www.rsa.com/en-us/company/news/the-dark-side-of-customer-data
7. https://www.accenture.com/us-en/insights/strategy/generation-purpose
8. https://www.forbes.com/sites/andriacheng/2019/06/20/mcdonalds-first-major-acquisition-in-years-could-be-a-game-changer/?sh=22a5c9c2361d
9. https://www.accenture.com/us-en/insights/strategy/reimagined-consumer-expectations
10. https://www.emarketer.com/content/most-consumers-creeped-out-by-ads-that-follow-them-across-devices
11. https://www.ox.ac.uk/news/2021-01-13-social-media-manipulation-political-actors-industrial-scale-problem-oxford-report
12. https://investor.fb.com/resources/default.aspx
13. https://www.theguardian.com/uk-news/2018/mar/23/leaked-cambridge-analyticas-blueprint-for-trump-victory
14. https://www.bu.edu/articles/2019/break-up-big-tech/
15. Ibid.
16. Ellyn Shook, Peter Lacy, Christie Smith, and Matthew Robinson, "Shaping the Sustainable Organization," Accenture https://www.accenture.com/us-en/insights/sustainability/sustainable-organization

Chapter 5

1. https://newsfeed.time.com/2012/11/01/banks-and-businesses-show-heart-in-wake-of-hurricane-sandy/
2. https://thecmoclub.com/cmo-perspectives/cmo-clubcast-with-accenture-humanizing-digital
   Source: CMO Club Clubcast Humanizing Digital 2021
3. https://www.davecarrollmusic.com/songwriting/united-breaks-guitars/
4. https://www.marketplace.org/2019/07/05/a-broken-guitar-a-youtube-video-and-a-new-era-of-customer-service/
5. Ibid.

Chapter 6

1. https://newsroom.accenture.com/news/majority-of-consumers-buying-from-companies-that-take-a-stand-on-issues-they-care-about-and-ditching-those-that-dont-accenture-study-finds.htm
2. Ibid.
3. https://www.businessinsider.com/oldest-companies-on-earth-2014-8
4. https://www.patagonia.com/core-values/
5. https://www.chick-fil-a.com/careers/culture
6. https://www.bls.gov/news.release/pdf/nlsoy.pdf
7. https://www.ibm.com/thought-leadership/institute-business-value/report/employee-expectations-2021
8. https://workinstitute.com/breaking-down-the-direct-costs-of-employee-turnover/
9. https://abcnews.go.com/Technology/wireStory/eruption-iceland-volcano-easing-affecting-flights-76577584
10. https://blog.klm.com/what-has-klm-learned-from-5-years-of-social-media-service/
11. https://www.business2community.com/social-media/social-media-case-study-klm-royal-dutch-airlines-066516
12. https://www.facebook.com/media/set/?set=a.448232065772&page=2
13. https://youtu.be/Sh-JRoY7_LU
14. https://research.aimultiple.com/chatbot-fail/

Chapter 8

1. https://www.apple.com/newsroom/2019/01/share-your-best-photos-shot-on-iphone/
2. https://www.youtube.com/watch?v=rq3n2sJ43Hg
3. https://www.usatoday.com/story/tech/talkingtech/2018/05/23/woman-charged-7-000-toilet-paper-amazon-refunded-2-months-later/637442002/
4. https://twitter.com/SanofiUS/status/1001824999496404992
5. https://twitter.com/MerriamWebster/status/724645568014868480

Chapter 9

1. https://thecmoclub.com/cmo-perspectives/cmo-clubcast-with-accenture-humanizing-digital
   Source: CMO Club Clubcast Humanizing Digital 2021

Chapter 10

1. https://www.livescience.com/2497-black-death-changed-world.html

Acknowledgments

I would like to thank Glen Hartman for his constant mentorship, encouragement, and support in writing this book. To my colleagues Mark Curtis, Jeriad Zoghby, and Gene Cornfield, I am grateful for your innovative ideas and thoughtful individual stories and perspectives. You really challenged my thinking throughout this process.

To Maureen McGuire and Corey Yulinsky, two of the best managers, thought partners, and friends I have had the honor to serve, who have provided invaluable support and guidance throughout my rather circuitous career journey. You always reminded me that "the proof of the pudding is in the eating."

To Amy Ondreyka and Mark Kiernan, whose efforts were invaluable in navigating this labyrinthine journey and who encouraged me to never surrender.

To Annie Knight, who chased me down and convinced me to finally put some of my thoughts to paper.

About the Author

Rob Harles is managing director and global head of the social media and modern channels practice for Accenture Song, responsible for consulting and building social strategies for the Fortune 1000. He joined Accenture from Bloomberg LP in New York where he was global head of social media, responsible for developing and managing Bloomberg's social media strategy and initiatives worldwide.

Prior to this, he was vice president of social media for Sears Holdings and built Sears' social media platform and customer communities. Before joining Sears, Rob spent 12 years working as a consultant building building growth strategies for the Fortune 500. He started his career at McKinsey & Co.

Rob has extensive experience building successful digital businesses in the areas of strategy, digital architecture and design, digital marketing, social media, and emerging channels. He also has specific expertise in artificial intelligence, machine learning, chatbot/digital automation, e-commerce, content marketing, and SEO/SEM, as well as the practical application of quantitative and qualitative analytics. Rob is passionate about ensuring that the human element doesn't get lost in technology.

Rob is a frequent speaker and writer on the future of digital innovation in customer care, knowledge management, marketing, and social media and is a regular speaker and panelist at conferences such as Social Media Week, Pivot, and the Digital Innovation Summit in New York City. Rob lived in the UK for 10 years and graduated from Oxford University with a BA and MA in modern European history.

Index